NEBRASKA BEER

GREAT PLAINS HISTORY BY THE PINT

TYLER A. THOMAS

AMERICAN PALATE

Published by American Palate
A Division of The History Press
Charleston, SC
www.historypress.net

Copyright © 2015 by Tyler A. Thomas
All rights reserved

Cover images: Windmill at sunset in Valentine, Nebraska. *Photo by Kelly DeLay*.
https://creativecommons.org/licenses/by/2.0; Fontenelle Brewing Company.
Courtesy of the Durham Museum photo archives, William Wentworth Collection.

First published 2015

Manufactured in the United States

ISBN 978.1.46711.780.7

Library of Congress Control Number: 2015947682

CONTENTS

CONTENTS

ACKNOWLEDGEMENTS

Thanks to The History Press and specifically Artie Crisp for taking a chance on this food blogger, giving me the opportunity to turn a hobby into something really substantial and something to be proud of. I appreciate your guidance, expertise and commitment throughout the entire process.

Thanks to the Nebraska brewers, homebrewers, distributors, beer sellers and beer drinkers and everyone else in the Nebraska beer business. It's because of your dedication to your craft and focus on doing what you do every day that I had the opportunity to pull this book together.

Thanks to each of the current brewery owners, head brewers and their staffs for taking the time to meet with me so that I could learn firsthand about your business and your experiences affecting the beer culture of Nebraska today. Your stories, determination and true grit inspired me to write this book and helped me get through some very tough late nights.

Thanks to the Nebraska State Historical Society, Adams County Historical Society and the Durham Museum for your help in untangling the web of history, as well as your continued dedication to preserving our state's historical data.

Thanks to Bill Baburek of Infusion Brewing for letting me raid your historical collection of Nebraska beer memorabilia on more than one occasion. And thanks to Mollie Cox for helping me photograph the collection.

Thanks to Amber Wolff for proofing, editing and helping me tell this story from a cohesive voice and ensuring that my tenses were correct. Your guidance and assistance were invaluable, and I'm not sure how I can pay it back.

ACKNOWLEDGEMENTS

To my wife, Mandy, thank you for your love, support, motivation and constant reassurance that I could complete this project. Even when I was ready to throw in the towel, you were there to boost me up and help this first-time author get through to the end. I appreciate your willingness in allowing me to sacrifice family time to pursue my passion. I am eternally grateful that I had you riding shotgun in this wild ride of a project.

AUTHOR'S NOTE

The stories included in this work are, to my knowledge, the most accurate and current. However, as we all know, things change and evolve quickly these days, and breweries are no exception. It is recommended before heading to any of the businesses included that you first call or check their company websites. Included in each section are both the phone number and website addresses for your convenience.

INTRODUCTION

When I first launched my food blog, nebraskafoodie.com, in the fall of 2012, I could never have foreseen the culinary adventure it would take me on. As a self-proclaimed foodie, I took to writing, photographing and sharing my experiences in efforts to give local businesses a little publicity. Fast-forward two years, and what started out as a hobby of eating, tweeting and blogging has turned into an extended journey across the state to uncover the unique stories, motivations and histories of the exploding Nebraska brewing scene.

Rooted in rich history, Nebraska brewers have played integral roles in the state since it was a territory. Now the art and science of brewing beer has reemerged on the prairie. Local entrepreneurs—each with different motivations, inspirations and recipe books—are taking the deep dive and starting their own breweries so we as beer drinkers can reap the benefits.

In this project, my journey led me across the state to meet individually with Nebraska brewers and business owners for a chance to uncover their stories. Each chapter highlights the unique history, people and personalities of a brewery or brewpub, paired with an overview of the beers it brews. The sections conclude with my favorite part: the history of the business name. While some names are obvious, others have a rich history, motivation or obscure background that make for a great story. Some sections also include another layer of history: the story behind the names of some of the beers sold.

While drinking my way across the state, I had the chance to learn, taste and explore styles of beer that I had never heard of or could have ever

INTRODUCTION

imagined. From styles rooted in tradition to coffee-infused beer and yummy brown beers, today's Nebraska brewers are brewing beers that rival those from big cities, and there are plenty of opportunities to enjoy them. From drinking in the taproom to beer festivals and six-packs in the grocery store, Nebraska brewers are providing local beer-drinking experiences that are putting the state on the craft beer map. And while our number of breweries and breadth of distribution might not compare to Denver's or Portland's, it has never been a better time to be a beer drinker in Nebraska. Breweries here are educating Nebraskans on craft beer and transforming consumers into craft beer drinkers, one pint at a time.

1

NEBRASKA BEER

A BRIEF HISTORY

Early explorers of the West considered Nebraska part of the "Great American Desert"; with no trees and little rainfall, the land was seen as a place of no return. The land was much later explored and settled by frontiersman, who had a sense of determination and a passion for independence. It was these attributes that contributed to their dedication to overcoming the large obstacles of turning the new unadulterated land into something that could support them and their families. It was their labor of the land and drive to make something for themselves that laid the groundwork for a Great American Desert to become a national and global player in agriculture production.

Coming from settled parts of the eastern United States and crowded areas of northern Europe—mainly Germany and Scandinavian countries, as well as Bohemia, Russia, England and Ireland—these frontiersmen entered an unknown world of treeless prairies and a landscape that they had never before experienced. Through their resourcefulness, drive and determination, they began transforming the prairie into something of which they could be humbly proud. According to historian Dorothy Weyer Creigh, still today "Nebraskans reflect the qualities of their pioneer fathers—the stubbornness that would not let them be defeated, the friendliness and generosity that makes no man a stranger on the prairie. Nebraskans possess audacity tempered with caution, honesty and trust, creativity, ambition, and most of all, force, determination and drive."

In 1854, before the Kansas-Nebraska Act of 1854 officially organized the territory of Nebraska, there were limited white settlers in the area. Settlers were mostly military forces along the Platte River and at Fort Laramie, as well as some fur traders and missionaries along the Missouri River who conducted business from the Iowa side of the river. However, by 1854, traders, explorers and other businessmen had started moving west across the river to strengthen their own business endeavors. Under the Federal Townsites Act, they could secure 320 acres of land for a town and then make a fortune by selling lots of the land in the new territory.

Historian Dorothy Weyer Creigh stated in her book *Nebraska: A History* that "by May, three weeks before President Pierce signed the Kansas-Nebraska bill, Iowa Congressman Bernhart Henn got a postmaster appointed for Omaha, and by May 28, 1854, A.D. Jones's log cabin was built." As soon as the territory was organized, log cabins were being built and saloonkeepers were setting up shop; Omaha was officially getting started.

Farmers were also starting to settle the western land. Before the land was even open in the territory, settlers were scoping out ideal locations, and as soon as the Kansas-Nebraska bill was passed, hundreds of immigrants sprinted to the area, setting up cabins and shanties to hold their stake in the land.

By the time the Nebraska territory was born, the American railroad era was beginning. At the end of the Civil War in 1865, construction on the Union Pacific Railroad began, and anyone available rushed to Omaha to help build a steel path across the plains of the Nebraska Territory. At any given time, four to five hundred men were laying the track across the uninhabited land moving west—at the end of each leg were end-of-the-rail communities. These tent communities were portable and sprang up every few hundred miles, moving along with the railroad crew. Nicknamed "hell-on-wheels," saloonkeepers, prostitutes, gamblers and people of all kinds would set up shop as the crew worked, and as workers completed one stretch of the line, they would move ahead and set up shop again. By 1867, when Nebraska became a state, the construction of the Union Pacific Railroad stretched completely across the state.

By 1869, the Burlington and Missouri River Railroad had begun a second line in the state, this time a southern route west of Plattsmouth. By 1873, the line stretched westward for two hundred miles and joined the Union Pacific mainline at Kearney Junction. While the Burlington was stretching west, the group focused on colonizing the area, and cities west of Lincoln were established, including Crete, Dorchester, Exeter, Fairmont, Grafton, Harvard, Inland, Juniata, Kenesaw and Lowell. The focus was no longer on pop-up towns like those of the Union Pacific but rather on villages and permanent settlements to build markets for the newly established railroads.

With new ways to make it out west, the railroads started to promote and develop the markets for future railroad traffic and launched promotional campaigns in eastern American cities and in northern Europe.

Hundreds and eventually thousands of homesteaders came to the area even before the rails were complete, taking the train as far west as it would take them, getting off and walking with all of their possessions to find an area that had good soil, was close to water and was not already claimed. As the rail lines were completed as far west as they went, new towns sprang up; Nebraska's expansion and mass migration seemed to happen almost overnight. As these communities started building houses and establishing commerce and governments, they also started launching common business enterprises like newspapers for sharing local news, flouring mills to convert the farmers' wheat into flour and saloons to quench the thirst of community members.

Saloons were some of the earliest enterprises in each community because of the need to know what was happening in town and the need for a place for community members to gather. Each community had plenty of carpenters, laborers, farmers and cowboys who, at the end the day, wanted a way to cool down and relax from their labor-intensive day. For many European immigrants, alcohol was a normal part of their daily routine.

As a larger group of immigrants from England and Germany made its way to Omaha to work on the railroad and to start the journey west, Nebraska started seeing breweries pop up across the state.

In 1859, Fred Krug of Cassel, Germany, opened Nebraska's first brewery in a one-story frame building, twenty-two by forty feet, on the south side of Farnam Street between Tenth and Eleventh Streets in Omaha, Nebraska. Each week, the brewery turned out 12 to 18 barrels, with most being sold to the Mormons at Florence. Within a few years, the brewery had outgrown its location and required a much larger capacity. In 1867, Krug erected the first brick brewery in Omaha at the southeast corner of Jackson and Eleventh Streets. By 1880, the Fred Krug Brewing Company was Nebraska's largest brewery, producing 25,000 barrels annually. In 1891, business growth led Krug to a more extensive and modern plant. The new location, housed on eighteen acres of ground, was purchased between Omaha and South Omaha; he built a plant with a capacity of 150,000 barrels of beer per year. In 1891, the business was incorporated as the Fred Krug Brewing Company.

In 1864, brothers Frederick Sr. and Phillip Metz bought the McCumbe Brewery and started the Metz Brothers Brewing Company. The German American Metz brothers built the business into a beer empire. The brewery was one of the most modern at the time, the facility took up an entire city block and beer was delivered by horse-drawn carriage.

In Saratoga, Nebraska, Saratoga Brewery was opened, but it was sold in 1863 and 1865 and later became Columbia Brewery. In 1876, Gottlieb Storz, a German immigrant, moved to Omaha and in 1884 purchased Columbia Brewery from the previous owner's widow. He moved the brewery to Omaha and renamed it Storz Brewing. Seven years later, Gottlieb formed Omaha Brewing Association and named himself president. Storz was an award-winning brewing company, with medals in 1898 and 1905 in international competitions in both Omaha and Portland. In 1892, Storz built a state-of-the-art facility in North Omaha, and the company saw great success until Nebraska's statewide prohibition took effect in 1917.

Willow Springs Distillery resided in Council Bluffs, Iowa, in 1866, but after a default on nonpayment of taxes, the federal government seized the business. A man by the name of Peter Illerof Wooster, Ohio, along with James Megeath and John McCormick, bought Willow Springs at auction and moved it across the Missouri River to Omaha, making it the first distillery in Nebraska. A year later, Iller and his brother, Joseph, moved to Omaha. By 1871, Willow Springs was making 6,000 to 7,000 gallons of alcohol per day, or 1.25 million gallons per year. By 1887, Willow Springs had become the third-largest distillery in the United States, producing 12,000 gallons of alcohol per day, which amounted to $3 million in sales. It employed 125 men, with an $80,000 payroll, and was paying more than $200,000 in federal taxes. Willow was a huge part of the local economy at the time, purchasing about 700,812 bushels of grain per year. In July 1898, Willow Springs was sold and became part of the Standard Distilling and Distributing Company.

DURING THIS TIME, South Omaha was becoming famous for one of the world's largest stockyards, and immigrants from all over the world were packing the house to work. One, Balthas Jetter from Germany, made his way to Omaha in the later part of the nineteenth century and had the intention of opening a brewery in Omaha. In 1887, along with a partner, Mr. Young, Jetter and Young Brewery was established at Thirtieth and Y Streets in South Omaha. At the time, Jetter's annual capacity was an impressive 10,000 barrels, and by 1890, Jetter had purchased full rights to the company and renamed it South Omaha Brewing Company. The business kept up its production pace, and with the growth of the packinghouse industry, production was increased to 30,000 barrels annually by 1902. In 1905, the brewery was known as Jetter Brewing Company, and after the turn of the century, it launched the brand Gold Top. An advertisement from 1902 read, "[A]lways snaps and sparkles, that never leaves a bad effect, that is a good beverage and a better tonic, that is Gold Top." In 1909, the brewery dropped Gold Top and led with a new brand, Old Age, brewing this beer until Prohibition. At its peak, Jetter Brewing Company turned out 100,000 barrels annually.

Outside Omaha, breweries were popping up and serving as community-gathering places. From areas like Columbus, Hastings and Crete to Falls City, Grand Island and Nebraska City, breweries were a common sight across Nebraska's frontier. The Columbus Brewing Company was founded by Charles Bremer in 1863 and was built on the corner of Seventh Street and Fifteenth Avenue. Bremer sold the brewery in 1876, and it was again sold in 1902.

The Hastings Brewery was owned and conducted by Theodore Bauersock, who was previously the foreman in a St. Louis brewery where Budweiser beer was brewed. Bauersock reported that the Hastings Brewery was an extensive manufacturing enterprise in 1887, making between five hundred and six hundred barrels of beer each week and shipping to all points in the state, as well as Kansas, Colorado and Wyoming.

However, while many breweries were scattered across the plains, others did not last for more than a handful of years. While each saloon and brewery

Hastings Brewery, Hastings, Nebraska. *Courtesy of Adams County (Nebraska) Historical Society Photograph Collection.*

was supplying stocks of beer and liquor to the community members, they were not without scrutiny and constant controversy.

From even before the days of the Nebraska territory, there were prohibition laws. The national Indian Intercourse Act of 1834 forbade the "disposing of spirituous liqueur" to Indians, and in 1855, the first Nebraska territorial legislature passed "an act to prohibit the sale and manufacturing of intoxicating liquor." However, neither the act nor the law was enforced, and in 1858, the legislature reversed its act and enacted a law permitting the granting of liquor licenses.

From the earliest decision to allow the manufacturing and selling of alcohol in the state, the discussion of prohibition in Nebraska was a constant issue in state politics, as well as a moral and emotional issue for residents. Many saw the evil of saloons and alcohol and blamed liquor for many of society's problems. On the other side of the table were the large breweries and distilleries across the state, as well as a large number of ethnic groups, all of whom accepted alcohol and saw prohibition as a threat to their traditional values.

For more than forty years, the topic of prohibition was discussed in state and local campaigns, and for twenty years or so, the Prohibition Party of Nebraska was active in the movement. In 1881, the first victory for the group came in the passage of the Slocumb Liquor License Law, which put operating fees on saloon owners. The law put a $500 minimum license fee on cities of not over ten thousand people, as well as villages, and not less than $1,000 in cities of the first class and cities having over ten thousand people. While this was seen as a victory for the party, the saloons had no trouble paying the fees and continued raking in the dough, operating without losing steam.

For the following decades, prohibition was a constant political topic, and many laws were passed to limit sales of alcoholic beverages, but they continued to fall short of outright prohibition. During the late nineteenth and early twentieth centuries, the city of Lincoln had a strong temperance movement, with members believing saloons to be evil institutions that challenged family values. However, the city also had groups that believed that drinking in moderation was fine and saw nothing wrong with a social life.

At the time, the Lincoln newspaper saw the saloons as a threat to democracy, as it believed that residents voted in favor of what the saloons wanted and ultimately saw saloons and breweries dominating local and state politics. Lincoln, like many cities across the state, was divided over the prohibition topic, an issue that broke down by ethnic group, social class, religion and the overall desire for political reform. The prohibitionists, or "drys," were usually residents of affluent neighborhoods and members of the city's professional and business elite. They tended to be in the upper socioeconomic classes and were strong churchgoers. Ethnicity also played a role, with many native-born American residents associating with the "drys."

Stereotypes were also common throughout this time, as many saw foreigners and African Americans as going hand in hand with saloon and brewers' interests. Those against prohibition were known as the "wets" and were usually from less affluent areas and represented the working class.

In 1902, Lincoln prohibition supporters were able to pass a progressive excise tax for city saloons and also limit their hours of operation to from 7:00 a.m. to 7:00 p.m. But the prohibitionist weren't done there. The battle continued.

In 1909, the "daylight saloon bill," which would limit saloon hours to 7:00 a.m. to 7:00 p.m., made it to the governor's desk. This type of bill had already passed in Lincoln, and prohibitionists were ready to make it state law. Then governor Ashton Shallenberger's stance on the bill was unknown, so he was inundated with petitions and strong lobbying from both groups. Former governor William Poynter urged Shallenberger to condemn saloons. The Lincoln newspapers were also convinced that Omaha saloons and breweries were the leading forces against the daylight saloon bill. At the time, the brewing industry had great power, as many of the malt liquor breweries had consolidated, building larger companies and employing more and more residents. Charles Metz of Metz Brewing declared that "if the very life of the city is not to be throttled, this bill must not be signed," according to "The Battle Over Alcohol" on the NebraskaStudies website. He threatened to lay off his labor force if the bill were signed.

Despite strong opposition to the bill by brewers and residents, the bill passed, narrowly, on April 3, 1909; shortly afterward, the bill was signed into law. This was the tipping point for the temperance movement, as its adherents still wanted a total ban on alcohol. The group got its wish: in 1916, Nebraska voters approved a statewide prohibition. By law, there would be no more alcohol manufactured or sold in the state starting in 1917. The United States followed suit when national Prohibition was secured by the passage of the Eighteenth Amendment in 1919.

NEBRASKA BEER

PROHIBITION

President Herbert Hoover called Prohibition the "Noble Experiment." Many thought the idea of eliminating alcohol abuse and keeping families together seemed positive, but it was soon seen as a failed experiment, as many across the country didn't see anything wrong with drinking alcohol in moderation. Many voters across the county thought that they were voting for the repeal of hard liquor and did not realize that beer and wine would also be outlawed. With passage of the Eighteenth Amendment, it was up to Congress to set the maximum alcoholic content in beverages. The Volstead Act put the maximum ABV percentage at .05 percent. Beer today has a significantly higher alcohol content at 4 to 6 percent on average, and whiskey is around 50 percent.

With Prohibition happening across the country and the new limits on maximum alcohol content, many Nebraskan breweries went offline. Other, larger breweries started brewing other beverages like near beer, which contained less than the .05 percent alcohol allowed by law. They also started producing soft drinks and other carbonated beverages. Storz Brewing Company began producing near beer, ginger ale, soft drinks and ice to help stay afloat as a company and save as many jobs as possible. Jetter Brewing similarly turned to producing near beer and soda, which drastically cut its production and negatively affected its workforce. The former Columbus Brewing Company also converted its operation to brew near beer and ice.

At the same time, Congress and the states were left with figuring out how to prohibit the public from making and consuming alcohol. Gin was now being brewed in bathtubs, and organized crime was on the rise. With the ban on alcohol production and consumption, the Omaha area saw a rise of speakeasies and hidden saloons. These hidden saloons also started to become popular destinations across Nebraska. As the Great Depression hit, the thought of being able to put people back to work in breweries started sounding like a good idea.

In 1932, newly elected president Franklin D. Roosevelt used his political power to repeal the Eighteenth Amendment. Congress agreed and sent the repeal to the states. While many states, thirty-six out of forty-eight, voted to ratify the repeal in 1933, Nebraskans did not vote to repeal the state's constitutional prohibition until 1934, doing so with a 60 to 40 percent margin.

Past Prohibition

With the repeal of Prohibition in 1934, Storz began brewing again and soon reached its peak, producing 150,000 barrels of beer annually. This amount of production helped Storz to become a household name and eventually become Nebraska's biggest seller. Storz often used the great outdoors to advertise its product. It was also popular for the hundreds of workers it employed, as well as its focus on giving back to the Omaha community through civic engagement.

In 1966, the family sold the business to Grain Belt Brewery of Minnesota, and the brewery operated in Omaha until its closure in 1972. In 2013, two Storz family relatives, cousins Tom and John Markel, decided to revitalize the brand and open Storz Trophy Room Grill and Brewery in Omaha's downtown riverfront. And while the cousins don't have the original recipes of their fathers and grandfathers, the new full-bodied Storz is brewed with the pre-Prohibition product that won international awards in mind. The Storz name today adorns an expressway, a hospital pavilion, the Joslyn Art Museum fountain court and other public areas.

The repeal of Prohibition also brought Falstaff Brewing Corporation to Omaha. The St. Louis, Missouri–based company purchased Krug Brewing Company, which made it the first brewery to operate plants in two different states. The Omaha plant helped Falstaff Brewing Company debunk the

Storz Brewing Company delivery trucks in front of the plant in 1946. *Courtesy of the Durham Museum photo archives, Bostwick-Frohardt/KMTV Collection.*

Three Storz warehouse men standing near a conveyor belt of Storz beers. *Courtesy of the Durham Museum photo archives, Bostwick-Frohardt/KMTV Collection.*

A Falstaff worker adjusting a valve in the plant. *Courtesy of the Durham Museum photo archives, William Wentworth Collection.*

A Fontenelle Brewing Company delivery truck with a Robin Hood Beer sign on the side. *Courtesy of the Durham Museum photo archives, William Wentworth Collection.*

Men working in the bottle house at Fontenelle Brewing Company in Omaha, Nebraska. *Courtesy of the Durham Museum photo archives, William Wentworth Collection.*

myth that the same beer couldn't be produced in different plants. With rigid controls on the process in Omaha, Falstaff was able to create a process that would be later copied by other national brewers.

During this time, Fontenelle Brewing Company established a plant at 210 Hickory Street in Omaha and brewed and distributed authentic Depression-era Robin Hood and Metz beers, both favorites across Nebraska. Fontenelle brewed from 1933 to 1938 and then closed. Metz then took over the space until 1961.

From the boom of breweries in the early days of the territory to a near extinction due to Prohibition and the Great Depression, Nebraska breweries have had a wild ride. In 1978, the federal government made homebrewing legal across the country, and many Nebraskans took up the hobby. With limited access to breweries and craft beer in the state, beer enthusiasts were left to brew their own beer. The hobbyists even formed homebrewing clubs, where members would bring batches of their latest recipe, try them out and critique them.

With a homebrewing foundation and a national trend of breweries and brewpubs opening, Nebraska in the early 1990s started taking baby steps toward national recognition in the craft beer world, but it wasn't until the mid- to late 2000s that we would see the surge of what we experience across the state today.

2

EMPYREAN BREWING COMPANY

729 Q Street, Lincoln, Nebraska 68508 | 402-434-5960
www.empyreanbrewingco.com | Founded in 1990

The Brewery

Founded in 1990 and opened in 1991, Lazlo's Brewery and Grill was Nebraska's first brewpub, and for the past twenty-five years, it has been the cornerstone of the Lincoln Historic Haymarket District.

With previous restaurant and service industry experience, Lincoln natives and brothers Scott and Brian Boles and their best friend, Jay "Lazlo" Jarvis, thought that they could bring their expertise to Lincoln. After traveling on the West Coast and experiencing the brewpub concept, they thought it would be exactly what they needed—something new and exciting that wasn't being done in Nebraska.

While the brewpub concept was working well on the coast at the time, there were no laws in Nebraska that would allow for it to come to fruition here. After Boles and Jarvis spent a few years working with Nebraska state legislators and leveraging their established relationships, the Nebraska state legislature voted and approved the establishment of brewpubs in the state in 1988, as noted on the website for the Nebraska Liquor Control Commission.

With the brewpub concept approved, the three moved forward with finding the future home of their business. Scott Boles became the liaison for the group and was in charge of scouting the location. Boles started looking to the Historic Haymarket, which at the time didn't have many businesses and was primarily an abandon warehouse district. The Haymarket location was a gamble, but so was the concept itself, as well as the idea of brewing beer that wasn't just lite beer.

After looking at multiple spaces, a recently renovated building at 710 P Street owned by Lou and Gale Shields became available. Boles put his sights on the space, and after negotiating with the Shieldses, the location became home of Nebraska's first brewpub, Lazlo's Brewery and Grill.

When first designing the business, none of the partners was a brewer by trade, or even a homebrewer for that matter. However, as good businessmen they knew they could find the right talent to run that arm of the business. After finding the local Lincoln homebrewers club, they went in search of a beer specialist.

At the time, Rich Chapin, an accomplished and award-winning homebrewer, was organizing the homebrewing competition for the Nebraska State Fair and running a bike shop after realizing that being a broker wasn't for him. Rich previously had experience interning in breweries in Europe and spent time in British Columbia researching brewpubs. He was the linchpin the trio was looking for. After learning about Rich, one day Scott went to his bike shop. After a conversation, Rich closed up his shop and Lazlo's had its head brewer.

After securing a head brewer, a location and a concept, they were off to the races. Right out of the gate, Lazlo's Brewery and Grill was packed. It even ran out of beer on the second day of business. Luckily a few additional batches were soon ready.

From day one, Lazlo's management made its customers the primary focus of its business; it even drafted a list of "Lazlo's Laws" that has been prominently located on the front of its menu for the past twenty-five years. Laws include, "This restaurant is run for the enjoyment and satisfaction of our guests, not the convenience of the staff or the owners," and, "Absolutely nobody should leave here upset or disappointed. If we fail to satisfy you, for any reason whatsoever, we want to know. The staff and owners are here to listen and help. That's what we get paid for."

The Lazlo's Laws and superior food quality and service have helped keep the forward momentum over the years. As the demand for Lazlo's food and beer grew, so did the business, and in 1997, Lazlo's sister company, Empyrean Brewing Company, was born. In 1996, the Lazlo's leadership began construction on a new fermentation cellar in the adjacent Coffee and Spice building at 729 Q Street, and in 1997, Empyrean beer started distributing beer in both Omaha and Lincoln. In 1999, after customer feedback and the experience of making a great brown beer, Empyrean bottled its first beers and launched with THIRD STONE BROWN.

Until this time, Rich had been brewing all the beer himself, but after 1999, four employees were hired. As Empyrean continued to expand distribution statewide in 2002, additional Lazlo's locations were also opened; with the increase of restaurant growth, there was a parallel growth of beer sales. In 2001, the Empyrean team tore the block apart and upgraded from its seven-barrel system to a fifteen-barrel brew house. This upgrade doubled its production speed and allowed it to bottle on a larger scale and at higher efficiency levels.

Since 2002, Lazlo's Brewery and Grill has opened two other locations (South Lincoln and West Omaha) and another brewpub concept, Fireworks. Each brewpub sells Empyrean ales, and to this day, all of the beer for all four locations and distribution is brewed at the Historic Haymarket site. With all walks of life enjoying a meal at Lazlo's or Fireworks or a pint from Empyrean in another restaurant, the company is quietly doing things right. It makes high-quality, consistent products tying the passion of the brewery back to the restaurant. For the past twenty-four years, Empyrean has been a destination for craft beer, laying the groundwork for Lincoln's craft beer scene.

THE BEER

From day one, Lazlo's Brewery and Grill sold homebrewed craft beer. It wasn't until 1997 that Empyrean Brewing Company became a separate business entity and started brewing and distributing all of the beer for Lazlo's and Fireworks locations.

From the beginning, all of the beer had been produced on the foundation of Rich's old-school English styles. When Lazlo's first opened its doors, there were four beers on tap, which at the time was a big deal. The beers included golden ale "SHOOTING STAR," a good training beer that featured local honey; an amber ale; a stout, "COLLAPSE R"; and a seasonal rotator. For most of the '90s, this lineup introduced Nebraskans to the idea of craft beer.

With the success of the original three beers and the start of outside distribution in 1997, Rich and his team developed additional award-winning

Third Stone Brown fresh off the bottling line. *Courtesy of Empyrean Brewing Company.*

beer recipes. Some of the original recipes were renamed, building the popular year-round lineup of beers available today.

The Shooting Star, renamed CHACO CANYON GOLD (4.8 percent ABV), is an easy-drinking golden ale with Nebraska honey and has a crisp hop finish. I think it tastes awesome with the classic Lazlo's Rainbow Chicken.

The LUNA SEA ESB (6.3 percent ABV) was updated in 2001 from the original amber ale and has been a staff favorite for twenty-four years. It even won the 2006 World Beer Cup Extra Special or Strong Bitter category.

The Empyrean brown beers are fan favorites and make up 40 percent of all beer sales. The THIRD STONE BROWN (5.3 percent ABV) is a smooth, dark beer that proves that not all dark beers are filling. This brew was the first beer developed under the Empyrean name and the first one sold in a bottle. The DARK SIDE VANILLA PORTER (5.7 percent ABV) is an Empyrean best-selling beer, roasted with hints of coffee, chocolate and vanilla. I love to finish off a meal with this one—it's my dessert.

The COLLAPSAR OATMEAL STOUT (5.6 percent ABV), BURNING SKYE SCOTTISH ALE (5.3 percent ABV) and WATCH MAN IPA (6 percent ABV) round out the year-round Empyrean brews.

An ode to "seize the beer," Carpe Brewem is an Empyrean Brewing Company trademarked line of beer. *Courtesy of Empyrean Brewing Company.*

Along with the year-round beers is the limited-edition "Eccentric Line" of seasonals, like the popular ARIES MARZEN OKTOBERFEST (5.3 percent ABV), available from September to November. This selection has hints of corn, bread and caramel with citrus hops. I enjoy this one the most with smoked turkey at Thanksgiving. The SUPER NOVA SUMMER FEST (5 percent ABV), FALLEN ANGEL SWEET STOUT (5.6 percent ABV), DOMINO EFFECT TRANSITION ALE (5.6 percent ABV) and WINTER AXIS FESTIVALE (6 percent ABV) round out the Eccentric Line.

The CARPE BREWEM limited-release lineup is Empyrean's ode to "seize the beer" and includes the latest traditional and sometimes not-so-traditional recipes from the brew crew. This lineup is a chance for the brewers to get a little wild and stretch their creativity and is available in four-packs at select locations across Nebraska.

With a constant demand for its beers, Empyrean has limited availability with which to experiment. However, to help combat the space issue, for the past eleven years it has been sponsoring a homebrewers competition, Beer

Quest, with the winner having his or her beer featured in Lazlo's restaurants. The contest has not only allowed Empyrean to give back to the community and connect with homebrewers, but it has also provided a platform for local homebrewers to elevate their recipes and gain some notoriety. And while most Beer Quest winners do not stay on the menu for too long, one particular beer, the MANGO IPA, went over so well that it is now available all the time and will likely be in bottles in the coming months.

While the Empyrean business model is to brew beers that pair and sell well with its restaurant food, it does have a few items in the works for the "beer nerds." From experimenting with cask beers and hosting cask beer nights the first non-holiday Monday of the month to barrel aging with tequila, Empyrean is staying up with the trends and providing something for all palates, even if it is in limited release.

If you're new to the world of craft beer, Empyrean has been hosting Beer School since 1998; it's a free, informal gathering where people can show up and try a few beers that are popular at the time from around the world. Usually there is a theme, and it is an opportunity for guests to learn more about Empyrean ales and craft beer as a whole. The idea originally started as a training concept for servers and bartenders, but it has exploded over the years and usually hits max fire code capacity of 150.

Empyrean ales are available at all Lazlo's and Firework locations and also at many other bars and restaurants across Nebraska, North and South Dakota and Iowa. You can also find an Empyrean selection at local grocery and liquor stores and craft beer bottle shops.

What's in a Name?

While doing research into the history of beer, the brew crew found that many ancient civilizations spent time watching the sky, monitoring the movement of planets and stars and thinking about how these movements affected life. These same civilizations also brewed beers. With all of the myths and stories and the potential to do a lot of cool things from branding to marketing and naming, the group knew that this would be an idea gold mine for their business.

Once it settled on the celestial theme for its brewery, it looked at launching with Big Bang Brewing Company—it is how the world started, and the group was attempting to make a "big bang" in Nebraska. However, research revealed that the name was already trademarked in California.

Back to the drawing board, Rich Chapin at the time recommended Empyrean, but the team immediately thought that it sounded hard to spell. After looking closer at the meaning, though, and seeing that Empyrean was a place in the highest heavens and was supposed to be occupied by the element of fire—it was heavenly and celestial—they thought they might as well give it a shot. The fiery symbol with the stylized *E*, designed by one of Brian's family members, has been the mark of Empyrean since inception. It has stuck to its celestial theme, diving into mythology, ancient civilizations and folklore when naming each of its new brews.

3

UPSTREAM BREWING COMPANY

514 South Eleventh Street, Omaha, Nebraska 68102 | 402-344-0200
www.upstreambrewing.com | Founded in 1996

THE BREWERY

Growing up in Lincoln and working in the restaurant business and, more specifically, the hotel business at the Cornhusker Hotel, Brian Magee knew that he liked the industry. After working himself up through hotel management, he knew that he could open his own restaurant and be successful at it. While visiting his brothers in Denver, Colorado, in the late 1980s, Brian came across the brewpub concept, and it immediately sparked his interest.

Returning from Colorado, Brian started doing his own research on the restaurant/brewery and pieced together how he could do it in Nebraska. With only a few other businesses doing this type of concept, namely Lazlo's in Lincoln and Jones Street Brewery and Sharky's in Omaha, he knew that the idea could work.

Continuing to research how to make his dream a reality in Nebraska, Brian came across John Hickenlooper, then owner of Wyncoop Brewing Company in Denver, Colorado. Hickenlooper was starting to partner with people across the country to expand the Wyncoop brewpub concept in other states. After connecting, Brian and John became partners and started searching for a space in Omaha for what would be their brewpub, Upstream Brewing Company.

At the time, the Old Market in downtown Omaha, Nebraska, was starting to resurrect itself. With the desire to have a building with character, Brian started searching in this part of town for a space. After looking at a few buildings, none was really right for what they wanted to do. It was by mere happenstance that Brian got word at a dinner party of a building in the heart of the Old Market that the current owners wanted to offload quickly. The building at the time was being used for a dinner theater, and after a tour of the space, Brian knew that it was perfect for his business venture.

The building, dating to 1904, was a former Omaha firehouse and still has evidence of its interesting past: the current second level houses the barracks, and from the main level, you can still see the holes in the ceiling from the fire poles. Since the closing of the firehouse, the building had previously been a garage, a warehouse and a dinner theater. Needless to say, this building had a great character and the right amount of space to be the home of Upstream Brewing Company.

After renovating the building, Upstream Brewing Company opened its doors in 1996. When Upstream first opened, food was sold exclusively on the main level, and the upstairs was more of a bar and lounge, with twelve pool tables and bar seating. On any given weekend, there was usually a line down the stairs and out the door—one in, one out—for the first few years of being open. While Upstream Brewing Company was a brewpub from the beginning, it wasn't until the end of year three that Upstream made the decision to really kick its food up a notch, hiring seasoned executive chef and partner Gary Hoffman. A Culinary Institute of America graduate, Gary came on board and carved the path for Upstream to quickly sell more food and, in turn, more beer. And this momentum has not let up in the past fifteen or more years. Upstream continued to grow and expanded to a second location in West Omaha in 2004.

As a staple restaurant and brewery in Omaha, Upstream continues to introduce guests to the idea of craft beer through its gateway of excellent food and superior service. Upstream is constantly renovating its space to fit the consumer demand and evolving its menu—not losing focus on the pub fare but rather adding more modern items and some interesting items for foodies. And with an extensive variety of beers always on tap, it continues to educate guests on craft beer one year and one beer at a time. The Upstream crew actively does its part to increase the population of craft beer drinkers.

The Beer

In 1996, when Upstream opened its doors, it started with five beers on draft and featured a pretty limited number of styles. It opened with standard introductory craft beer styles like pale ales, Scotch ales, brown ales and ESB. Well, Upstream's beer selection has changed dramatically. Its production has exploded, and there is now a great variety to what is available on any given day.

From the seven house beers that are always available—"O!" Gold Light Lager (3.8 percent ABV), Raspberry Lager (3.8 percent ABV), Capitol

A prominent stream is included within the Upstream Brewing Company logo. *Courtesy of Upstream Brewing Company.*

PREMIUM PALE ALE (5.5 percent ABV), FIREHOUSE RED ALE (5.0 percent ABV), FLAGSHIP IPA (6.4 percent ABV), DUNDEE EXPORT SCOTCH ALE (6.6 percent ABV) and the cask-conditioned ales—to the large variety of rotating seasonals, there is a beer for every palate at Upstream.

In 2014 alone, Upstream Brewing Company rotated in forty-eight different beer varieties, not including its cask- and barrel-aged selections. And with limited distribution outside the two brewpubs, that is a ton of beer. With no "typical" customer, Upstream is constantly introducing newbies to the art of craft beer, yet its taps are also flowing with variety for the beer aficionados.

Under the direction of Dallas Archer, head brewmaster, the team combines passion with science and art in each barrel. Deriving inspiration from traditional styles, local ingredients, the seasons and special events, the brew crew at Upstream knows that it cannot satisfy everybody, but it can provide a large variety. From the Non-Dallas Micromanaged Series, in which the brewers have a chance to exercise their own creativity, and the cask-conditioned beers served at cellar temperature of fifty to fifty-five degrees to a beer engine and barrel-aged beers available in 750-milliliter corked and caged bottles, Upstream Brewery has a variety for everyone.

WHAT'S IN A NAME?

Upstream's name is derived from the meaning of the Native American word *U-Mo'n-Ho'n*, or "Omaha," which was given to those Native Americans who broke from their tribe and went "upstream" to settle the new area. Keeping with the historical relevance of the great city of Omaha and with the idea that it takes water to make great beer, Brian thought that Upstream Brewing Company was a great name for the business.

4

SPILKER ALES

300 West Fourth Street, Cortland, Nebraska 68331 | 402-798-7445
www.hopluia.com | Founded in 1996

The Brewery

Cortland, a village in Gage County, Nebraska, is home to fewer than five hundred people and to Nebraska's hoppiest brewery, Spilker Ales.

Sam Spilker, a naturally curious fellow, grew up in Cortland, Nebraska, and it was during his high school and college days that he first dabbled in homebrewing. Not completely sold on brewing just then, he left for Colorado State University. While in Fort Collins, Colorado, he truly fell in love with good beer.

It was no surprise that in attending college at the boom of H.C. Berger Brewing Company, Odell Brewing Company and New Belgium, Sam would become a huge fan of good craft beer. It was during his final year in college that he seriously began thinking about what was next for him and his biochemistry degree. It did not take long for the light bulb to go off, and he decided that he should open his own brewery.

At the time, there were few resources at his fingertips, so he started diving into books about brewing and rediscovered homebrewing, making it a permanent hobby. After finishing school and with his degree in hand, Sam moved back to Cortland, Nebraska, and did everything in his power to self-finance his dream of opening his own craft brewery.

Doing what he had to do to make his dream a reality, he began sourcing scrap stainless steel dairy tanks and converted them into working brewing equipment. He sourced enough scrap parts and worked with a local welder to figure out the perfect configuration for what would be his unique brewing system.

Back in Cortland in 1994, Spilker moved into a building that had formerly been a bank that went out of business during the Great Depression and later became a grocery store. The building's former bank vault had been transformed into a walk-in cooler and was perfect for Sam to use as he started his new brewery. For a year and a half before selling his first beer, Sam worked part-time jobs, remodeled the building and continued looking for scrap stainless steel parts, getting everything ready for brewing.

Diving into the deep end, this self-taught brewer with few physical resources applied what he had read in his research. Through many rounds of trial and error and a little learning the hard way, Sam Spilker opened Spilker Ales, selling his first beer in December 1996.

When he opened the doors for the first time, Spilker Ales had seven different beers on tap. Based on some reviews of his products, it became apparent that people weren't remembering the beers they were trying at the brewery. So, Sam decided to scrap six of his beers and put all of his focus on just one beer. With just one beer to focus on, Sam thought he could better manage his batch size and efficiency and focus on getting really good at brewing one style of beer. At the time, HOPLUIA was his best seller, so it was a no-brainer that this would be his bread and butter; it was for eleven straight years.

A self-proclaimed "hop freak," Sam loves the bite and aroma of hops and enjoys experimenting with them in many different ways. He has even tried smoking them out of a pipe (true story). From rubbing hops and using both whole and pelleted hops in his recipes, Sam has built a brewing system in which he can solely focus on developing the three elements of hops (bitterness, flavor and aroma), and he experiments with every variety through processes unique to Spilker Ales.

Each year, Spilker Ales brews on what Sam has nicknamed his "Frankenstein" brewery equipment. His brewery, which is primarily self-financed, features thirty major pieces of equipment, with only three originally designed for beer. The other secondhand pieces have been sourced from dairies, creameries, farms, scrap yards and various other sources and have all been cobbled together to build out the Spilker Ales brewing system.

From his great-uncle Ben's circa 1920 roller mill, still used to mill the malt, to three old champagne tanks that feature ⅜-inch-thick shells that can hold

A view of the milk tanker that Sam Spilker of Spilker Ales converted for his brew house. *Photo by the author.*

pressure that would normally blow up most brewery tanks, Hopluia takes its time working during secondary fermentation. The "Frankenstein" brewery system also features a fermenter converted from a rolled-over milk tanker from Des Moines, Iowa. A semi truck milk tanker got in a bad accident, so Sam bought the destroyed vehicle for $1,000, sold off some of the scrap metal for $1,500 and converted the remainder into his 5,800-gallon fermenter that he still uses today.

With its home-built system and focus on one style of beer, Spilker Ales brews and sells about six hundred barrels each year. Selling exclusively in Omaha and Lincoln on tap at nearly eighty bars and restaurants, a "Frankenstein"-brewed beer is not too hard to come by. Hopluia is also available in twenty-two-ounce glass bottles at many craft beer retailers and grocery stores. It has so much hoppy goodness from the finished hops that a bottle laid on its side for a month will have the effect of turning the underside of the bottle cap slightly green. Strange but true!

THE BEER

With a laser focus on one type of beer, which can mostly be described as a Belgian pale ale, Spilker Ales is able to do that one style and do it really well. With no other products in its line, it can focus on perfecting its unique dry-hopping method, which some describe as "truly bizarre." Hopluia is brewed using a rare method of dry hopping that works in the secondary fermentation and is brewed with two different yeast strains. The result is a hoppy beer of immense taste.

When it comes to drinking Hopluia, it is a golden pour with a white head, features a citrus aroma and has great flavor. It is a perfect day-drinking beer, and when it is served super cold, you could not ask for a better beer with hop flavor. As I am a huge fan of hops and hoppy beers, Hopluia has been my constant go-to, up until recently with the release of Spilker Ales' latest creation, SONAR.

For the past eleven years, Spilker Ales has only brewed and distributed Hopluia to the Nebraska market. In March 2015, it released a whole new product called Sonar. With few hop varieties that really had standout aroma and flavor around fifteen to twenty years ago, Spilker Ales had stayed away from releasing another line. Fast-forward to the present day, and there are

Until 2015, Hopluia was the only beer that Spilker Ales brewed. *Courtesy of Spilker Ales.*

The first three variations of Sonar were released by Spilker Ales in 2015. *Courtesy of Spilker Ales.*

twenty to thirty varieties, all of which have great aroma, flavor and taste. With plenty of other varieties yet to be discovered, Spilker released Sonar, an ever-changing brew with mind-bending hops.

By sampling a ton of different hops on a small scale and discovering those with the perfect characteristics and flavors to complement one another, Spilker Ales can build out unique batches featuring two different hops that are introduced during its key dry-hopping phase. It will roll out a completely new batch of beer each time Sonar is brewed. The line was kicked off with three different batches; every forty to sixty days, a new batch will make it to the market and will feature a completely different variety of hops.

I sampled the first three batches of Sonar and can tell you that since each batch used a completely different array of hops, the flavor and aroma of each was a surprise on the palate, giving a good mouth feel and taking you on a flavor roller coaster. I cannot wait to be surprised by each new batch of Sonar and hope that I can try each variety, one pint at a time.

WHAT'S IN A NAME?

Not all breweries can have long histories and detailed stories of how their founders came up with the name. Some breweries, like their humble founders, just keep it simple and choose a last name and a popular beer style to name their brewery. This is the case with Spilker Ales.

Sam Spilker decided to open his brewery in his hometown, and he named it after himself. Not much more of a story here. The Spilker Ales beer names, however, have their own unique little tales.

The Gospel of Hops

Hopluia is nicknamed the "Gospel of Hops." *Courtesy of Spilker Ales.*

Hopluia (pronounced like "hallelujah") is a play on words with no religious context. Founder Sam Spilker just hoped that people would shout his beer's name from the mountaintops as they would "hallelujah." That's why it's nicknamed "the Gospel of Hops."

The newly released Sonar plays off the idea that your nose, like a sonar, will ping the different aroma "waves" of hops from each truly unique batch and excite your taste buds. With a completely new variety of hops in each batch, the hope is that your nose will detect each distinct aroma and ultimately take your nose on an aroma adventure.

5

THUNDERHEAD BREWING COMPANY

18 East Twenty-first Street, Kearney, Nebraska 68847 | 308-237-1558
www.thunderheadbrewing.com | Founded in 1999

THE BREWERY

After seven years in the air force and a short stint as a garbage truck driver in small-town Nebraska, Trevor Schaben decided that he did not like what he did every day. With an entrepreneurial sprit, he decided to start his own business.

During his time in the air force, he had visited beer capitals of the world in Germany and Belgium and had the chance to explore many West Coast breweries. An avid homebrewer himself, Trevor realized that with so many good beers out there and with no breweries in the area at the time in Nebraska, making beer was a perfect chance to make a living doing something he wanted to do.

After quitting his job as a garbage truck driver in Gothenburg, Nebraska, Trevor headed to Davis, California, to attend the American Brewers Guild's five-week brew master course at the University of California–Davis. After his quick crash course, Trevor returned to Nebraska and settled on opening Thunderhead Brewing Company in downtown Kearney, Nebraska. At the time, he was living in Gothenburg but thought that Kearney was the most viable option for brewing and selling the beer he would brew.

Trevor started Thunderhead Brewing on a one-barrel system, brewing nine times a week. After some recipe experimentation, dumped barrels and working out the kinks, he quickly perfected his recipes and was open just three to four days a week; oftentimes he would run out. Running out of product was a great issue to have, but it is hard to make much money to run a business off just small batches.

After just six months of being open, Thunderhead purchased a three-barrel system, and Trevor began brewing ninety-three-gallon batches; he quickly realized that his current location was not ideal for what he wanted to do. Moving just a few blocks from the original Thunderhead location, he gutted a new building to fit a future seven-barrel brew house, as well as a kitchen on the second floor. With no original intentions to run a brewpub, Trevor knew that having a restaurant would keep Thunderhead competitive and allow it to make additional revenue.

In the new space, Thunderhead continued to crank out a ton of beer, pushing twelve barrels on a newly acquired seven-barrel system. After about four years of pushing hard, Trevor had a friend build out the perfect space for a production facility in the neighboring town of Axtell, Nebraska. In 2011, the town of barely three hundred became the new home of Thunderhead Brewing Company's production facility.

The new space included room for forklifts, a canning line and all of Thunderhead's brewing equipment. The Axtell production facility allowed Thunderhead to reach a new level of efficiency and stay competitive. In 2015, it started giving free brewery tours. Guests on Saturday afternoons can swing by for a sneak peek to see where the magic happens, along with free samples and an opportunity to buy cases of beer directly from the source.

Thunderhead Brewpub is open seven days a week and is definitely a family affair. Trevor produces all of the wort himself and is in the process of training an assistant brewer. Trevor's dad, David, is the warehouse manager and builds orders and moves trucks around. Trevor's mom, Pam, helps with the bookkeeping, and Trevor's wife, Jenny, helps with marketing. This family vibe is felt throughout the brewpub, and it was set up that way intentionally. The Thunderhead Brewpub is a family drinking environment, with customers often bringing their kids and grandparents with them when they stop by. On any given day, there are all types of customers swinging by for a pint, from bikers to priests; you see all walks of life at Thunderhead. Trevor would be happy just making beer. But the people really dig his place, and he digs that.

The Beer

When Trevor first launched Thunderhead Brewing, he had just finished brewing school and wanted to spend time learning a lot about the ingredients and the brewing process. He spent time diving into the brewing world and bought grain, yeast and hops from anyone and everyone, exploring his options and experimenting with beer styles.

Oddly enough, honey wheat was available in the early stages of the business, so Trevor brewed it a bunch of different ways for the first six months. It was during this time on the one-barrel that he developed categories of beers that would allow him to ease in the new crowd of craft beer drinkers but not limit his creativity or variety. The categories he developed included varieties of light beers (wheat, fruit, pilsners and kölsch) to start, specifically for the craft beer newbies. Other categories included red and amber beers, black beers and bitter beers.

Once Thunderhead graduated to the three-barrel system, it needed regular customers, and with regular customers came regular favorites that needed to be available. At the time Thunderhead Brewing was just kicking the boots off craft beer, many of the locals had not heard of or experienced craft beer before.

Sticking to his categories, Trevor refined his recipes and launched fan favorites like the Golden Frau Honey Wheat (7.5 percent ABV), a wholesome wheat beer brewed with sweet Nebraska Sandhills honey. From the beginning, this beer has been and continues to be a fan favorite.

The Leatherhead Red Ale (5.2 percent ABV) is an English-style red ale that's dry-hopped with Willamette flowers. This red ale is one of my favorites; with an amber color, thin white head, roasty aroma and slightly dry bitter finish, it's the perfect brew for Nebraska game day.

The Schaben's Pilsner (5 percent ABV) is a German-style pilsner that is step-mashed and fermented cold, and the Cropduster IPA (6.5 percent ABV) is an aggressively hopped cascade IPA balanced with full-flavor two-row barley. The Cornstalker Dark Wheat (5.2 percent ABV) is a dark American wheat brewed with malted Nebraska corn. I am not huge fan of dark beer, but this is surprisingly mellow and enjoyable. Other Thunderhead year-round beers include the Prairie Peach Wheat (5 percent ABV), Grail Ale Grand Cru (6.5 percent ABV) and the Jalapeño Ale (4.95 percent ABV).

Along with the year-round beers are a fun bunch of seasonal beers and two new series that Trevor is trying out. In January 2015, Thunderhead started its barrel-aging program, with barrel-aged beers set to become available in

Golden Frau Honey Wheat features Nebraska Sandhills honey. *Courtesy of Thunderhead Brewing Company.*

The Thunderhead Brewing Company Leatherhead Red Ale is nicknamed the "Grid Iron Ale." *Courtesy of Thunderhead Brewing Company.*

early 2016. It also launched the small-batch Cellarman Series, with which it can try out unique recipes like the Medieval Scottish Ale and the Spiced Apple Cider and sell them exclusively in the brewpub.

Most of the year-round Thunderhead brews are currently available in cans and are distributed across Nebraska, South Dakota, Iowa and Kansas. Thunderhead also distributes draft beer through a unique partnership with the Chicken Coop Sports Bar, and you can find Thunderhead beers on tap at Chicken Coops in Grand Island, Nebraska, and both Urbandale, Iowa, and West Des Moines, Iowa.

WHAT'S IN A NAME?

When contemplating a name for the business, Trevor knew that he needed something "cool." With a lot of experience living on the coasts and flying while in the air force, thunderstorms were something that often caught his attention. After moving back to the Midwest, he thought that there was just something unique and intense about these types of storms. Liking the idea of Thunderhead Brew House, it was Trevor's wife, Jenny, who suggested Thunderhead Brewing. With a slight play on words from "thunder is brewing" and "thunder clouds brewing," it made sense that this would be the name for the business. He decided on Thunderhead Brewing Company.

Thunderhead Brewing is a play on the idea that "thunder is brewing." *Courtesy of Thunderhead Brewing Company.*

6

SCHILLINGBRIDGE WINERY & MICROBREWERY AND SCHILLINGBRIDGE CORK & TAP HOUSE

Winery & Microbrewery
710 Road, Pawnee City, Nebraska 68420 | 402-852-2400
www.schillingbridgewinery.com | Founded in 2005

Cork & Tap House
575 Fallbrook Boulevard, Suite 109, Lincoln, Nebraska 68521 | 402-904-7161
www.schillingbridgecorkandtap.com | Founded in 2014

The Brewery

Located in Pawnee City, a Nebraska town of roughly 850 people, is the United States' first operating farm winery and microbrewery to ever be housed in the same facility. Owned and operated by serial entrepreneurs and business owners Sharon and Mike Schilling, this facility sits on thirty-five acres right outside town.

When thirty-five acres of land became available in the late 1990s, these longtime Pawnee City residents purchased it and began farming. After growing corn and soybeans for a while, on a whim they decided that they would transform the land and build out a winery. With plans for contract grape growing, they also thought that it would be best to provide a place where you could not only enjoy a nice glass of wine but also grab a great beer.

In 2005, after a year and a half working on sorting out the correct licenses with the federal and state governments, SchillingBridge Winery & Microbrewery was born. With a homebrewing background and love for beer, Mike Schilling initially started contract brewing with Omaha-based Upstream Brewing Company for a year and a half before building out the full-service SchillingBridge brew system.

With a plan of "revitalizing rural America, one beer at a time," the Schillings built a twelve-thousand-square-foot facility featuring a wine and beer tasting room and banquet facility and laid out a plan to increase tourism to their tiny town. In 2005, the SchillingBridge Edelweiss wine won a double gold in an international wine competition, putting the winery on the map. Tourists started making the trek to Pawnee City from Omaha and Lincoln for the award-winning wine and were surprised and delighted to find that they could order great beer, too! Naturally, as more and more people discovered SchillingBridge Winery & Microbrewery, the business began to boom, and the number of distribution accounts grew from three to eighty-seven in just nine months for both beer and wine.

With the Schillings being naturally fun people, they wanted to make each guest experience a memorable one in addition to selling a great product. From unique events like their comedy event Corned Beer and Comedy, held during St. Patrick's Day weekend, to Murder Mystery dinner theaters, with professional actors flown in from Chicago, the Schillings are selling out events. Tourists are showing up in Pawnee City in droves. One of the most successful events even garnered national attention: the over-twenty-one Easter egg hunt. For the event, the Schillings hide four thousand eggs across fifteen acres of their vineyard, and teams of adults flock to the field in search of the eggs. Each egg is filled with candy, drink coupons and other prizes, and teams compete for a chance to win a full case of wine or beer. Needless to say, the competition is fierce, and the event attracts more than four hundred people each year.

Even with unique events and great customer service, the recession affected the Schillings, too, and they started to look at additional ways to get their beer and wine to their loyal guests. After the recession had eased, and also after three years of new licenses and paperwork, Mike and Sharon's son, Dallas Schilling, and daughter, Kelly Bletscher, opened SchillingBridge Cork & Tap House in Lincoln, Nebraska, in September 2014. This separate family business brews its own small-batch specialty beers in addition to offering SchillingBridge wine and big-batch beers.

Located five miles north of downtown Lincoln, Nebraska, in the Fallbrook neighborhood, SchillingBridge Cork & Tap House is not your typical restaurant or taproom; it calls itself a wine- and beer-infused gastropub.

When Dallas and Kelly were designing the business, they wanted to focus on serving food that included their family's wine and beer in the cooking process. They developed a menu that not only features typical bar food (burgers and flatbreads) but also has a breadth of recipes, like their wine-braised beef, made with SchillingBridge Right O' Way red, and the pork chop with an extra pale ale cheese sauce–covered baked potato. The SchillingBridge Cork & Tap House aims to bring a whole new flavor profile to guests, with the opportunity to not only order a pint of its beer but also taste that same beer in its offerings like the Scottish ale beer bread or possibly the California common beer cheese.

Similar to SchillingBridge in Pawnee City, the Cork & Tap House is serving up delicious beers and building community through custom community events. From the Rhythm and Brews summer music festival to the weekly live music on the custom-made 1,700-square-foot patio, the Cork & Tap House is winning over the Fallbrook neighborhood and catering to the Lincoln community. The space is quickly becoming a neighborhood hot spot, but in the meantime, "tourists" are still continuing to flock to Pawnee City and escape the city life. It is estimated that over the past ten years, SchillingBridge Winery & Microbrewery has seen more than 200,000 guests, and it hopes to see that number continue to rise over the coming years.

The Beer

SchillingBridge's big-batch beers can be summed up in just a few words: great sessional beers. It does not get too funky with its recipes, and most are under 5 percent ABV. The Schillings strive to develop very drinkable beers that appeal to the masses. Their hand-crafted beers are inspired by what they like to drink and generally what the public wants. Each of the big-batch beers is brewed in the Pawnee City facility and distributed throughout Nebraska and are also available on draft at the SchillingBridge Cork & Tap House in Lincoln.

The SchillingBridge sessional beers include an extra pale ale (4.8 percent ABV), a California common (5.0 percent ABV), a Scottish ale (5.0 percent ABV), an American pale ale (5.8 percent ABV) and a roasted wheat (5.3 percent ABV).

The roasted wheat is by far my favorite SchillingBridge beer. They finish this beer with orange rind and lemon grass, adding a perfect citrus flavor and crisp finish. With slight notes of pine, this is a perfect pint.

A display of SchillingBridge beer varieties. *Courtesy of SchillingBridge Winery & Microbrewery.*

SchillingBridge also has a chocolate stout (6.8 percent ABV), which is both smooth and rich but not too sweet. The unsweetened chocolate and roasted coffee flavors help to keep it balanced. It's definitely an after-dinner drink but not something you couldn't finish, like some stout beers.

The SchillingBridge India pale ale (7.3 percent ABV) is another standout, as it has prominent hop bitterness, but it is not overpowering like some standard IPAs can be. This is definitely an IPA to try if you typically do not care for IPAs.

While most of the beers served at both SchillingBridge businesses are brewed in Pawnee City, small-scale cask beers are brewed at the Tap House in Lincoln. Also in Lincoln, they tap a new small-batch cask beer variety once per month. These more creative batches are geared to entice the beer nerds of the area and expose novice drinkers to something new. One of the latest varieties is a dark roasted beer, aged in a SchillingBridge Oak Chamourcin wine barrel with three and a half pounds of toffee, three pounds of unsweetened cocoa nibs and one and a half pounds of sweet hops. It has a roasty, dark, oaky coffee flavor, and on top is the complexity of the toffee and dark chocolate. It is like biting into an unsweetened chocolate bar. With the opportunity to brew small-batch varieties, I expect SchillingBridge Cork & Tap House will continue to amp up its creativity and happily surprise us each month.

What's in a Name?

The SchillingBridge Winery & Microbrewery is set on thirty-five acres, and trains used to run right through the property. Still prominent on the property is the circa 1890 limestone Rock Island Railroad Bridge, which links Pawnee City to its railroad past. The Schillings paired this notable property fixture with their last name and established their business as SchillingBridge. To this day, the bridge sits right down from the vineyard; at almost fifteen to twenty feet high, you cannot miss it.

1

SOARING WINGS WINERY
AND BREWERY

17111 South 138th Street, Springfield, Nebraska 68059 | 402-253-2479
www.soaringwingswine.com | Founded in 2004

THE BREWERY

From the ripe age of thirteen, Jim Shaw has been making alcohol, beginning with mulberry wine in his adolescence and moving on to homebrewing while living in Utah as a young adult. It was this hobby that sparked his interest in opening a brewery in the mid-1990s in the Dallas, Texas area. After running into issues with overall cost and the requirement to open a restaurant with his brewery, Jim ditched the idea. But in 1998, Jim and his wife moved back to the Omaha, Nebraska area to take care of their aging parents, and the idea of owning a winery/brewery was rekindled.

In 2001, Jim decided he was going to open a winery and bought the perfect land for growing grapes in Springfield, Nebraska. Situated on vertical acreage to grow the grapes, the winery is an ideal rural setting, with wild turkeys and deer, and it is easily accessible for those who live in Omaha, Lincoln and other surrounding areas.

After three years of planting, harvesting and processing, Soaring Wings Winery opened to the public in 2004. And after four successful years of selling wine, Jim tapped back into his homebrewing experience and decided to add a brewery to his business in 2009. Growing up in south

Soaring Wings is off the beaten path in Springfield, Nebraska. When driving the gravel path, look for this sign. *Photo by the author.*

Omaha and remembering the smells of Fallstaff Brewing, this seemed a natural progression.

Initially, Jim hired a brew master who worked part time developing recipes and brewing beer for the newly named Soaring Wings Winery and Brewery. After about a year with the brew master, Jim took over the brewing process and has been brewing all of the Soaring Wings beer himself for the past four years.

Adding the brewery component to the business made perfect sense from a business model standpoint, as having beer in addition to wine was key to attracting new customers for business activities and events. Uniquely situated minutes outside Omaha, Soaring Wings Winery and Brewery is a venue like no other. Predominantly an outdoor music venue, this family-friendly space can seat up to two thousand people.

With outdoor concerts throughout the year on Sunday nights and a Friday night concert series during the summer, Soaring Wings provides a unique environment for all. From families with small children to adults who want that adult-only feel, the venue is vast enough to create a unique experience for everyone. Beyond the weekend concerts, Soaring Wings hosts a yearly Spring Wine, Beer, Blues and Balloons Festival that annually attracts 1,200 to 1,500 people.

The Soaring Wings Winery and Brewery experience is like no other in the area. There is no other place so conveniently located in a rural setting that overlooks rows and rows of beautiful grapevines and sells both beer and wine made on site. It is a truly unique Nebraska experience.

THE BEER

From his early days of homebrewing with a brew kit in Salt Lake City, Utah, to his now seven-barrel tank capacity, Jim has been brewing a variety of workhorse beers that are perfect for his outdoor concert setting.

From the Low Level Lager (3.9 percent ABV), the White Stripe Wit (5 percent ABV) and the Pegasus Pilsner (4.5 percent ABV) to the Aviator English Ale (6.4 percent ABV) and the Blackbird (6.5 percent ABV) stout, Soaring Wings Winery and Brewery has a variety that stretches from low-level lagers through heavy dark ales. A number of the Soaring Wings brews are also gluten-reduced, providing beer options for those who may be gluten intolerant.

The beers at Soaring Wings are quite seasonable and are sold exclusively on site. Guests can enjoy beer by the pint or growler or even take a five-sample flight. The flights are served in a souvenir red wine glass. And while you might think that sampling in a wine glass is odd, the curved top actually helps keep the aroma in the glass.

One of the favorite Soaring Wings beers is the Imperial Stout (10.7 percent ABV). Sold only in a 750ml bottle, it is aged in Soaring Wings wine barrels for six months, and boy is this beer brutal. It has massive flavor and a real punch but also a delightful smoothness about it. With hints of cherry, raisin and a slight coffee flavor, it's a great bottle to take home and enjoy during a Nebraska thunderstorm.

The summer RASPBERRY WHEAT (4.5 percent ABV) is the perfect summertime German wheat with a hint of raspberry. When touring Soaring Wings, I had a chance to sample some freshly brewed, and it was delicious! I love the summer months, when this is regularly on tap.

Soaring Wings continually tries to keep fan favorites on tap, but Jim is known to mix it up and work in additional seasonal beers when there is time and space. A few past seasonal beers have included a WINTER SPICED ALE, full of vanilla, cinnamon and sweet orange; a BOMBADIER BROWN ALE, featuring coffee, espresso and chocolate overtones; and the SUN SPELL ALE, a summer Belgian ale.

No matter if you're visiting on a weekend in the winter or stopping by for a summer night concert, the selection at Soaring Wings Winery and Brewery is sure to please, and you can't beat the venue!

WHAT'S IN A NAME?

As a former air force pilot and current international airline pilot, flying is in Jim's blood, so it only made sense to give his business a flying theme. Originally, Jim wanted to name his business Silver Wings, but he was not able to due to an existing trademark. With that out, Soaring Wings was a close second and became the name adopted by the business. Extending the theme, Jim continues to weave in avionic influences when he names each of his beers, with popular beers like Aviator English Ale, Pegasus Pilsner and Afterburner Red Ale.

8

NEBRASKA BREWING COMPANY

Brewpub
7474 Towne Center Parkway, Suite 101, Papillion, Nebraska 68046 | 402-934-7100
www.nebraskabrewingco.com | Founded in 2007

Brewery & Taproom
6950 South 108th Street, La Vista, Nebraska 68128 | 402-934-7988
www.nebraskabrewingco.com | Opened in 2011

The Brewery

In the early '90s, Paul Kavulak had a successful day job in IT and never really thought about how the beer he enjoyed made it to the shelf in grocery stores. It was not until a co-worker invited him over to help with a homebrew that Paul started thinking about how the beer he enjoyed was produced. The first batch of beer he helped his co-worker brew was not anything special—actually, it was quite horrible. But it was this experience of homebrewing that sparked Paul's interest, and he has been homebrewing ever since.

For thirteen years, Paul continued to brew his own beer. Every now and then, he threw a twelve-hour poker tournament where he and his friends could enjoy his latest brews and he could empty out his supply so he could brew something new. During this time, Paul also joined a local homebrew club and started meeting other local Omaha craft beer enthusiasts. After a number of years perfecting his recipes, specifically the Cardinal Pale Ale, Paul knew that brewing and selling beer was something he wanted to pursue. The pale ale, named for Paul's grandparents' South Omaha bar of the 1950s was the catalyst for Paul and his wife, Kim Kavulak, to start building out their business plan for an Omaha-area brewpub.

At the time, Kim, a former IT project manager, was at home with their young children, and Paul was still working his day job. With their business plan in progress, an opportunity to purchase a brew house from a defunct brewery in Japan came about, and the Kavulaks jumped on it, having missed out on two previous brew house bids. With the brew house secured and waiting in storage, the two started to research different locations for their future brewpub and stumbled on an up-and-coming outdoor lifestyle center under construction in Papillion, Nebraska. With nothing else in that part of town, the two Omaha natives knew that the future Shadow Lake Towne Center near Seventy-second and Cornhusker would be perfect for the *Cheers*-like brewpub concept they were planning to build.

After meeting with the Shadow Lake Towne Center property managers, Kim and Paul discussed their dream of an Omaha brew house, deciding that it would never be more than a dream if they could not invest all of their time and attention into making it happen. It was during that same discussion that Paul pulled out his cellphone, called his boss and resigned from his full-time job.

With a new focus and no outside income, the two entrepreneurs dug in their heels. Within a short amount of time, Nebraska Brewing Company (NBC) brewpub was opened in November 2007. At the time, the brewpub opened with four standard NBC beers on tap and a food menu that would work hand in hand with the beer it brewed. The food was focused on pairing with craft beer and included pizza, burgers and sandwiches, all served in a casual environment. The brewpub environment allowed visitors a chance to belly up to the bar, eat at private dining tables or throw parties on the elevated mezzanine. And during the summer months, guests could enjoy favorites like the Grown Up Mac 'N Cheese while sipping a Brunette Nut Brown on the large outdoor patio.

During the business build-out, the future head brewer of NBC, Tyson Arp, was also making a career change from construction to brewing and was looking for a place to work. Tyson, an avid homebrewer, applied across Omaha for jobs, including NBC, with little luck. Tyson finally caught Paul's attention after winning Best of Show in the Nebraska State Fair homebrewing

The Nebraska Brewing Company brewpub opened in November 2007 in the Shadow Lake Towne Center in Papillion, Nebraska. *Courtesy of Nebraska Brewing Company.*

competition with his rye IPA, a contest that Paul judged. After meeting at the contest, Paul brought Tyson on as a volunteer assistant brewer to help out the NBC team and see what he could do.

During Nebraska Brewing Company's first year, the Great Recession hit the United States and started to take effect on area businesses; NBC did not go unscathed. As new business owners ironing out the natural kinks of launching a new service-oriented business and dealing with the economy, Paul and Kim began to feel the pinch. With sales flat-lining in the brewpub, NBC started to look for additional revenue streams outside the brewpub. Distribution was a natural extension of selling more NBC beer and did not rely on customers visiting the pub to make the sales.

Knowing that their beers were good but not yet great, Paul and his brewers invested time in testing, refining and correcting their beers and gearing up to handle heavier levels of distribution. During this rebuilding, refining and correcting of the NBC beers, Tyson was promoted to lead brewer and spent a year perfecting the brewery's products.

With Paul charting the path for Nebraska Brewing Company to make it out of the recession and Tyson focusing on the beer, Nebraska Brewing Company started to improve on every level of business. Between 2009 and

2011, the brewpub bounced back, and on the beer sales side, NBC was selling everything it could brew either at its pub or via outside distribution.

In 2011, with its beer sales doing well, a barrel-aged beer program underway and distribution to fifteen states, NBC embarked on construction and expansion of a new production facility and taproom, which opened in 2014.

Located in LaVista, Nebraska, just minutes from the brewpub, the new space allowed Nebraska Brewing Company to continue to meet demand and expand its reach to a variety of different customers. From educating and inspiring the beer novice who stops by the pub for a bite to eat, to providing for the beer enthusiast who swings by the taproom after work, NBC's facilities allow it to provide a superior product to all craft beer drinkers.

NBC also expanded the education and exploration of craft beer with its annual Great Nebraska Beer Festival. In its seventh year, the festival is all about the beer, brewers and attendees and brings together more than eighty-five brewers from across the country, allowing attendees to experience more than four hundred beers that many Nebraskans would not otherwise have a chance to try. The festival is another way for Nebraska Brewing Company to continue to build and foster the craft beer community and expose more people to the world of craft beer.

THE BEER

When Nebraska Brewing Company first opened its brewpub doors, it had four standard beers on tap and one seasonal brew it would rotate. From the beginning, the cornerstone beer of Nebraska Brewing Company was its CARDINAL PALE ALE (6.0 percent ABV). This award-winning American pale ale was how I was first introduced to Nebraska Brewing Company. It's crisp, with floral/citrus aromatics that are a result of the additional dry hopping of a very large amount of Cascade hops. I'm a big fan of hops, and this beer does not disappoint; it has a truly pleasing floral aroma, and it's very drinkable.

Growing from the original four, Nebraska Brewing Company now has seven standard beers and three seasonals available on draft and by the can; all are brewed with the goal of never underestimating the palate of the beer drinker. As beer drinkers first, the folks on the NBC team do not dumb down the beer just to sell it; their goals are to respect the beer and brew it the best they can.

Cardinal Pale Ale sits on pallet in the Nebraska Brewing Company facility, waiting to make it to your next barbecue. *Courtesy of Nebraska Brewing Company.*

With a strong focus on balancing flavors and brewing beers that are an experience in themselves, Tyson and his assistant brewers focus on brewing beer that is vibrant and not dull or muddy. They brew beer that makes you want to have another sip. One of the most recent NBC creations I tried was the standard ALE STORM (5.1 percent ABV), a perfect baseball or casual-time beer. Launched in 2013, this brew is a balance of pilsner malt and lemony/spicy notes of Sterling hops and pairs well with fan-favorite snacks like peanuts, hotdogs and crackerjacks.

Other standard NBC beers include the EOS HEFEWEIZEN (5.2 percent ABV), a Bavarian wheat beer; BRUNETTE STYLE BROWN (4.7 percent ABV), an English-style brown; INFINITE WIT (4.7 percent ABV), a Belgian wit; the HOPANOMALY (9.3 percent ABV), a blend of a Belgian tripel and a West Coast IPA; and the IPA (6.9 percent ABV). My favorite seasonal is the WICK FOR BRAINS PUMPKIN ALE (6.1 percent ABV), which includes real pumpkin, not just pumpkin spice. It's perfect during the wickedly cold Nebraska winter months.

NBC also has a barrel-aged series. In 2008, it first started experimenting with barrel aging and was one of the first breweries to embrace the wine barrel—not to sour the beer but rather to pull out the characteristics of the wine. From the original two oak Chardonnay barrels stored under the stairs in the brewpub to the seven varieties now in the Reserve Series, NBC has made a national name for itself in the category. The series includes the award-winning MÉLANGE A TROIS (11.3 percent ABV), a strong-style Belgian blonde ale that is matured in a French oak Chardonnay wine barrel. This particular beer won a Gold Award at the 2011 Great American Beer Festival and has continued to win awards. After the Reserve Series' success, NBC launched the Inception Series, which includes experiments from NBC's extremely limited-edition barrel-aged program.

Seventeen types of Nebraska Brewing Company beer are available throughout the United States (twenty-five states to date), with current exploration overseas as Paul and the team look to expand the American craft beer impact to countries abroad. And with eight taps at the brewpub and twenty-four at the taproom, Tyson continues to explore his war chest of recipes, piloting and exploring new unknown craft beer combinations. I can't wait to see what comes off the line next!

WHAT'S IN A NAME?

When planning their business, one of the first projects Paul and Kim undertook was developing artwork for their beers and designing a corporate logo. As they were brainstorming concepts for the business, they originally were inspired by Indian names and took to options like Flat Land, Flat Branch and Flat Water, as well as looked at names of a few defunct breweries.

Initially, the team settled on Flat Land and developed visual graphics to complement the name. However, after attending the Great American Beer Fest, they discovered another brewery and restaurant with the same name. Before a cease-and-desist could hit their doorstep, they decided to change their name.

When first trying to decide on a new name, they looked at names that could possibly be a letter-for-letter replacement from the original artwork commissioned, but they didn't have much luck. After throwing around other options, they reluctantly decided on Nebraska Brewing Company. Their reluctance was in whether they could represent the whole state. Would people buy beer from Nebraska? After getting over their concerns, the two moved forward with the name. The name, which was originally used by a

The Nebraska Brewing Company name allows customers to know who the brewery is and where the beer is coming from. *Courtesy of Nebraska Brewing Company.*

brewery from 1897 to 1898 and a contract brewery in 1994–96, was perfect for their business. The couple liked that they could tie their business back to their home state and also liked that there was relevance in place. Hearing the name, consumers would immediately know who they were and where the beer was from.

9

LUCKY BUCKET BREWING COMPANY

11941 Centennial Road, Suite 1, La Vista, Nebraska 68128 | 402-763-8868
www.luckybucketbrewing.com | Founded in 2008.

The Brewery

For many young people, when they head off to college, they pick a major and a potential career path and align their class schedules and activities to get themselves prepared for that career—especially if they are planning on going into medicine. For Jason Payne, it was no different; he came out of college with a bachelor's degree in biology and a minor in chemistry, and for much of his life, he had planned to attend medical school.

But when medical school did not pan out, he took a job with Cargill in Blaire, Nebraska, where he could use his science background, and began working in an industrial fermentation plant. He worked with corn gluten (sugar source) and yeast, and instead of making alcohol (like you do with beer), the process produced lactic acid, which would polymerize into a biodegradable plastic. In his role, he had to test and control fermentation processes and troubleshoot quite often to make sure that his end product turned out as planned. While this job paid the bills, Jason—a self-proclaimed "foodie" and lover of local food, craft beer, spirits and artisanal cheeses and bread—left after a year at Cargill to pursue his dream of entering the food and beverage industry.

GREAT PLAINS HISTORY BY THE PINT

To start out, Jason began cleaning kegs at Upstream Brewing Company, worked his way up to head brewer and served as its brewer for five years. During this time, he cut his teeth on making recipes and playing around with barrel-aged beers and even won a handful of awards. At the same time, he went back to business school for his MBA and started working on a business plan that would allow him to expand his recipe mix beyond the walls of the two existing Upstream brewpubs. With a business plan in hand, a few business partners and a first round of funding, Lucky Bucket Brewing Company was launched in November 2008 and sold its first beer in early 2009.

The goal of Lucky Bucket Brewing from the beginning was to build a production brewery that would allow for a wider range of distribution and ultimately get its product in front of more people, creating a bigger footprint in the craft beer industry.

At the time, there were a few craft brewpubs but no full active-production breweries in the general Omaha, Nebraska area. To get started, Lucky Bucket began looking for space to house its production facility, and during the search, it teamed up with SchillingBridge Winery and Brewery in Pawnee City, Nebraska, and set up an alternating proprietorship.

The proprietorship allowed Lucky Bucket to brew, filter and package from the SchillingBridge facility. After establishing this proprietorship, Lucky Bucket hit the ground running with promotions around the Omaha area. Four to five times a week it would tour the Omaha area, handing out samples of its product and telling people its story. Focusing on guerrilla-style marketing and social media, it moved to make a dent in the Omaha beer culture, with its number-one goal being to make its name resonate in the market. Its goal was achieved quickly, and after ten months at SchillingBridge, Lucky Bucket quickly outgrew its space. This speedy growth left the owners scrambling for investors to raise more capital and find a space to continue brewing.

After scanning the Omaha metro market, Lucky Bucket found the perfect home for its production brewery nestled in an industrial area just south of Omaha in LaVista, Nebraska. LaVista, the newest city in the state and one of the fastest growing, provided the perfect small-town atmosphere and was just minutes from I-80, a major thoroughfare. The LaVista location's more than eighteen-thousand-square-foot building provided a blank canvas for building out the business.

At the beginning of the build-out, Lucky Bucket was able to secure a used twenty-barrel tank from a brew house in Buffalo, New York, and continued with four forty-barrel tanks, five one-hundred-barrel tanks, a one-hundred-barrel bright tank and a maturation tank, plus its bottling and packaging area. The goal of a fully functional craft beer production facility had been accomplished.

While some might think that an industrial area is not ideal for customers to visit or experience the brand, that is simply not the case with Lucky Bucket. Thousands of people make the trip to the area each year to take a tour of the facility. Lucky Bucket encourages tours and guided exploration of its facility, allowing guests an up-close and personal view. Brewery tours offer a chance to meet one of the two head brewers, learn about what was brewed that week and hear the anecdotal stories or issues faced that week. The tours and production transparency offer customers a firsthand look at where its beer is produced and a chance to meet the hands that make it. This type of transparency creates a unique comfort level, offering an exclusive behind-the-scenes look at where and how a customer's beer is made.

Whether you're filling your growler, stopping by for a tour or attending a Lucky Bucket event, you will likely come into contact with one of the Lucky Bucket employees. This small team of craft beer enthusiasts is filled with local folks who wear a ton of different hats and fill a number of different roles. While the head brewer might brew your favorite beer, receive a shipment of labels or refill your glass in the taproom, all Lucky Bucket employees have one thing in common: they love craft beer, and you can see that through the twinkle in their eye. The Lucky Bucket family takes great pride in their product, knowing that their friends, neighbors and fellow community members will be the ones enjoying it. The team does whatever it can to enhance that brand experience and provide a sense of community.

Part of the active community building is through the events the brewery hosts. If tours aren't your thing or you want to stick around afterward, the Lucky Bucket taproom has been built out to provide a space to gather and try any of the beers on tap. Oftentimes, its small-batch beers are tested exclusively in the taproom. The space is also used for corporate parties and nightly after-work hangouts. With such a large facility and friendly neighbors, Lucky Bucket hosts four special events each year, inviting guests to experience the brand in a whole new way.

In the winter months, it hosts a Winter Blues Festival, focused on getting people out of the house and giving them something to do so they don't go crazy at home. As May rolls around, there is the Lucky Bucket Beer Run, a one-of-a-kind experience that is less about how fast you run and more about friends, hilarious costumes, drinking beer and having a great time. Each year, you have a pick of the difficulty of either a rugged 7k trail or 5k paved course, according to the organization's website. In mid-July, Lucky Bucket invites everyone out to a Summer Beer BBQ, featuring food, music and great beer; it's a post–Fourth of July blowout. And it raps up its yearly events in September with Octoberfest, where it sets up a 650-square-foot tent and pulls out a semi trailer with plenty of taps on the side. The event draws more than 1,200 people each year.

THE BEER

Whether you're attending an event or picking up a six-pack in the store, Lucky Bucket has a great staff with tons of ideas, and they try to feed their creativity with the beers that they brew. From the five year-round beers to the four seasonal options, Lucky Buckets hopes to find something that fills any niche out there. Its portfolio features beers that cover all of the big gaps as far as favorite craft beer styles: hoppy, big and roasty, malty, entry-level beers and a number of seasonal flavors to mix up your cooler.

The five year-round beers include the PRE-PROHIBITION STYLE LAGER (4.5 percent ABV), which features distinct flavor and provides a good bridge for those who have enjoyed traditional light beer. It's a nice amber lager with a good malty/hoppy balance. It is a clean and crisp beer.

The HEARTLAND WHEAT (4.8 percent ABV) is a traditional wheat beer made from water, hops, yeast and barley, but Lucky Bucket's has a fifth ingredient: golden wheat from the American heartland, as noted on its website. This brew has a great golden color, and for those familiar with wheat beers, it's a nice option.

The year-round beers round out with a traditional India pale ale (6.3 percent ABV) and the must-try CERTIFIED EVIL, an imperial porter (9.1 percent ABV). This brew is particularly wicked, providing bold flavors with aggressive hops and a massive malt profile. It's packed with flavor.

The Lucky Bucket seasonals are some of my favorites because, as with any seasonal, they are only available for a short time, so you can't ever get bored. My favorite summertime seasonal is the BELLY FLOP (4.5 percent ABV); available between May and July, it is the perfect strawberry blonde pale ale that you can enjoy on the lake or in the backyard. The flavor is created by the recipe's abundant use of the best American two-row malted barley and Pacific Northwest hops. The slight haze, strawberry aroma and flavor are

A collection of Lucky Bucket brews. *Courtesy of Lucky Bucket Brewing Company.*

infused into this beer by using 100 percent seedless strawberries nurtured by the California sun.

The Snowsuit (5.3 percent ABV), available between November and January, is a great winter seasonal, perfect for gifting over the holiday season or bringing to your family function. It is a spiced Belgian abbey ale, brewed in the traditional style that goes back centuries but with a fresh spin. The special blend of six spices perfectly accents the fruity notes derived from the traditional Belgian Trappist yeast, bringing out the flavors of the season.

Rounding out the seasonal options are the vibrant Belgian saison SPRINGBREAK (5.3 percent ABV), available between February and April, and then there is the authentic OKTOBERFEST lager (5.5 percent ABV) available between August and October. Oktoberfest is out just in time to end the summer and is ready for you to enjoy all the way through October.

Lucky Bucket's year-round and seasonal beers are available across Nebraska, North Dakota, South Dakota and parts of Tennessee, but its exclusive single batches are only available in its taproom. This is where Lucky Bucket brewers get creative and push their boundaries of hops, spices and sweet flavors. Each special batch is unique and worth the drive to the taproom. The team gets together and tweaks recipes to fit them in when possible. A few of their recent single batches included some explosive combinations.

When meeting with Jason, I tried the JUG THUMPER MALTY BROWN. This is the perfect beer for malt lovers! It was a little sweeter and featured lovely chocolaty notes. The UP IN SMOKE was a smoked-chili porter and featured smoked malts and chili powder, chili peppers and a little bit of spice on top of a traditional porter recipe. The WHISKEY BARREL AGED CERTIFIED EVIL was brewed in empty whiskey barrels from the Lucky Bucket distillery. The TOTAL RECALL was a traditional Belgian tripel that used the yeast from the Snowsuit winter seasonal; they brewed a tripel with it, the end result being a 9 percent traditional tripel-style beer.

No matter what type of craft beer you're looking for, Lucky Bucket's product portfolio is intentionally diverse, focusing on filling the niche gaps and creating something for everyone. And on the horizon for Lucky Bucket are more year-round beers, an expansion of its product portfolio and growing its footprint and impact on the craft beer world. This product expansion also includes a tasting room renovation to look forward to.

WHAT'S IN A NAME?

When Lucky Bucket was first starting out, the founders realized that both marketing and name recognition were going to be key in competing in the

The Lucky Bucket name plays off the past tradition of small towns having one brewery and community members bringing their pale or bucket to fill up at the local brewery. *Courtesy of Lucky Bucket Brewing Company.*

craft beer market. They knew that they needed a name that could stand out among the competition and be catchy and relevant.

After brainstorming a bunch of different names, they test-marketed Lucky Bucket with a number of focus groups. The name itself plays off the past tradition of small towns having one brewery and community members in that town going up to the local brewery with their pale or bucket to fill up and take the beer home. When they tested the name with the focus group, the people smiled. This was the reaction that the Lucky Bucket founders were looking for. Lucky Bucket was the clear winner for a brewery name.

10
MODERN MONKS

North Eleventh Street, Lincoln, Nebraska, 68508
www.modernmonks.com | Founded in 2010

THE BREWERY

In the oldest brewing facility in Lincoln, Nebraska, there are three monks. No, these are not your typical monks. They have no religious affiliation, they don't chant and none is chaste. They are three former homebrewers who have made a vow to brew kick-ass craft beer.

Each monk had a unique path to brewing. Dave Oenbring began homebrewing before it was even legal in the United States. Using his grandmother's equipment and recipe, he brewed his first batch in 1976, a few years before President Jimmy Carter signed bill H.R. 1337 making homebrewing legal in the United States in 1987.

Bob Myer started homebrewing in 1992 and in the early 2000s converted his garage into a sophisticated home brewery, including in-ground plumbing, floor drains and everything in between.

The final monk, Jason Ames, began homebrewing in 2006 after receiving a kit as a gift from his in-laws. An avid cook and lover of making things for himself, he found homebrewing to be a natural extension of his existing hobbies. It was not too long into his homebrewing process that he received a ninety-year-old handwritten note from his grandmother that featured a homebrewing recipe from his great-grandfather, who had been a homebrewer during Prohibition.

The three monks found one another in the local homebrewing club Lincoln Lagers Homebrew Club and officially formed an LLC in 2007. Shortly after establishing themselves, they began commuting back and forth to Grand Island, Nebraska, brewing out of the Thunderhead Brewing Company facility. Their first beer sold well, and it was not long until they were in their own facility in Grand Island at the Chicken Coop Brewery. In 2010, after a short stint at the Chicken Coop, the facility decided to go in a different direction; the monks were without a monastery and began their search for a new home.

After not being fully satisfied by a number of the craft beers at Misty's, a local Lincoln, Nebraska restaurant, the monks approached Misty's owners with an offer to be their new brewers. After a few months of relationship building and negotiations, the guys moved into Misty's production facility and released their first Modern Monk beer, an orange wheat, in May 2010. With the release of the orange wheat, the monks reformulated all of their recipes and became the principal brewers in all three Misty's locations in Lincoln, Nebraska.

As the second craft brewers in Lincoln at the time, the guys have been pushing the original 1992 WynCoup brewpub brewing equipment to its max, producing nearly five hundred barrels per year. Their impact on the scene has been evident, providing a superior craft beer product at one of Lincoln's most popular restaurants.

The monks have also helped put Lincoln and Nebraska on the map, with both Josh and Dave being certified beer judges by the Beer Judges Certification Program. This intense three-hour handwritten test (with no notes) requires that each person taking the test know every single style of beer and its origination, as well as the name of each classic style of beer, plus its bittering units, color, taste, flavor, aroma and so on. The strenuous test turned both Dave and Josh into self-proclaimed beer nerds, and it's their nerdery that directly affects the types of beer the monks brew.

THE BEER

The Modern Monks beer lineup is based on the original five beers that were available on tap at Misty's restaurants when the monks took over the brewery. And while the styles of beer are the same, they have been updated.

The five year-round selections include a kölsch, an American pale ale, Stonehenge Orange Wheat, an atbier and Robust Porter. Each of the year-round beers is brewed to provide something for everyone who comes to Misty's. No matter if you're enjoying soup, salad or a steak, you can find a local craft beer to help wash it down. The selection that Modern Monks brews is vast, covering all craft beer experience levels, and its seasonals provide a sense of creativity and playfulness for the more adventurous craft beer drinker.

The original Stonehenge Orange Wheat is by far my favorite of the year-round selections. The subtle orange flavor and coriander make this a highly refreshing and drinkable beer whether you're drinking this with your favorite Misty's burger or an Omaha steak.

While all five of these beers are available at each Misty's restaurant, they are also on tap at many popular Lincoln bars and restaurants. A small selection has been canned and is available at local grocery stores across Nebraska.

With the production equipment, production schedule and demand of the Misty's restaurants, occasionally the monks have a chance to work in a few unique

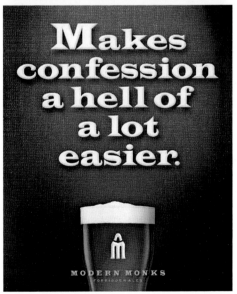

Modern Monks' advertisements and signage consistently play off their somewhat religiously affiliated brand name. *Courtesy of the Modern Monks.*

seasonal blends. Their extensive background in all types of beers includes a unique seasonal selection of a classic American pilsner, a Belgian IPA, an Irish red and a honey saison. They've even barrel aged a few small batches that they roll out every now and again. And while their barrel aged is good, the most unique seasonal that I have found is their oyster stout. Yes, oyster stout. It's a stout beer to which they add a boatload of shucked oysters from brine at a specific point in the process. The beer smells slightly briny, and it's robust and full. After you take your first swallow and breathe in, that taste of ocean air cuts across your palate. As I am not a stout drinker, I was a little hesitant when I first tried it, but I will admit that I'm a fan. It's definitely worth trying. If the oysters throw you off, forget about them and try it anyway.

The name Modern Monks pays homage to the original monks who brewed in years past. *Courtesy of the Modern Monks.*

The monks' homebrewing background gives them a very creative edge, and they deliver some excellent beers with unique flavors. They will never apologize if you do not like something, but they will definitely find something on tap that you will enjoy.

What's in a Name?

Since the Middle Ages, monks have been brewing beer. They are the original brewers and mastered brewing the same beer over and over with high degrees of consistency. At the time, they thought their beer was made from barley, hops and water (with a little help from God), but little did they know that their magical stirring sticks were transferring yeast from beer to beer.

It's because of this tradition of consistency that Modern Monks pays homage to the honor of the original monks who brewed in years past. As the monks are lovers of Belgian beer themselves, by adding modern techniques and equipment to the mix, the name Modern Monks made perfect sense for the group. It's an opportunity for these brewers to honor the tradition of those who came before them but add a modern twist on what they started.

11

BLUE BLOOD BREWING COMPANY

500 West South Street, Suite 8, Lincoln, Nebraska 68522 | 402-477-2337
www.bluebloodbrewing.com | Founded in 2011

The Brewery

"Stop! Put your hands where I can see them." That's something you might have heard Brian Podwinski shout if you had a run-in with him in the early 2000s. A Lincoln native and founder of Blue Blood Brewing Company, Brian was a police officer for five years with the Lincoln Police Department until an on-the-job injury led to his early retirement.

Following his retirement, Brian worked another government job, which led him to drink more. Well, actually, he spent more time tapping into his creative side, exploring the world of homebrewing. With his homebrewing kit, free time and space to try out new recipes, he started perfecting extra special bitter (ESB) recipes and experimented with different ingredients and formulas. Brian's tinkering and curiosity had him hooked. He shared this hobby with a friend (who was also in law enforcement), and together they began brewing (and drinking) more and more. Their hobby turned into two years of research, recipe planning and business plan writing, and ultimately, they opened the doors to Blue Blood Brewing Company in Lincoln, Nebraska, in December 2011.

The path to popping a can of Blue Blood was not the easiest. Brian and his business partners first had to work through many different banks to get someone to buy into their idea, and with some cash in hand, they found a new local bank that partnered to assist with the financial side of the business. With finances secured and equipment on its way, they needed to find a brewing space.

Brian and his co-founders knew that they wanted to be in an industrial area that provided plenty of space to brew, can their product and distribute. They had no original intentions of opening a taproom or owning really anything that resembled a bar. With their backgrounds in law enforcement, they figured that owning and operating a bar was not the best idea. After searching through many different industrial options in Lincoln, they found a location that provided reasonable truck access, space for employee parking and enough space for visitors to tour the brewery.

The 6,300-square-foot building was the prime location for a craft brewery, perfect for both brewing and distributing. At the original build-out, Blue Blood's taproom was just 300 square feet, but after the partners launched the business, the taproom exploded. The space became a popular destination for Lincoln residents and was quickly upgraded to 700 square feet to accommodate the growing demand.

The taproom serves as the perfect platform for customers of all walks of life to enjoy any of the sixteen beers on tap. On any given day, you could be bumping elbows with current Nebraska state senators, off-duty law enforcement officials, college kids or even retirees. The space allows Blue Blood Brewing to stretch its creative muscles and try out things it can't always just package and put on shelves, at least not right away.

The best part of Blue Bloods taproom is that visitors are not tied to just the beers that are distributed or the pints they are used to ordering at local bars. The taproom is the brewers' creative playground, and they are constantly trying new small batches. Visitors are welcomed into the world of brewing magic and exposed to the wide selection of the latest Blue Blood creations with the ability to taste-test new products and give immediate feedback to the brewers.

Like any great local business, it's rewarding to know that your favorite menu item will be there, but the most fun is knowing what you want and getting the opportunity to try the latest and greatest Blue Blood creation. The once-ignored space has quickly become a focal point of the business, from the packed taproom each weekend to private party rentals to the casual hipster or blue-collared folks who just want to enjoy a well-balanced local brew.

The taproom is where Gil, Blue Blood's head brewer, has a chance to test out his latest wild idea. Gil joined the Blue Blood crew as a young gun from Michigan, bringing new and fresh ideas to the brewery. Together with some other Blue Blood employees, all with homebrewing experience, he regularly develops new brewing concepts, keeping Blue Blood fresh and customer focused.

While the taproom is the creative playground, the brewery's focus is canning and distributing its product across Nebraska, Illinois and Iowa in local stores, restaurants and bars with hopes to expand into other midwestern states in the near future.

And did I mention that it cans its beer? Brian and the Blue Blood team spent a great amount of time doing research and weighing the pros and cons of canning versus bottling; to them, canning was the clear winner. As a new business, keeping the bottom line low was an obvious benefit of canning over bottling, as you can ship more cans than bottles. But it was not just for monetary reasons that Blue Blood chose to can its products. The benefit of having its packaging preprinted was a major factor, as well as not having to protect its cans like you have to with glass bottles. Blue Blood also wants its consumers to be able to take its product on the go. Whether you are biking, hiking or spending a day at the lake, throwing cans in your cooler, in most instances, is much easier and much safer, as you do not have to worry about glass clanking or breaking. Blue Blood also believes in the canning lifecycle: It put beer in cans. We buy beer in cans. We drink beer in cans. We return/recycle the cans. We then have more money to buy more cans of beer.

THE BEER

With the customer in mind, Blue Blood Brewing Company focuses on brewing well-balanced beers. As each new beer is being developed and tested, the flavors have to balance out. There can't be one profile that overtakes another or becomes extreme. The Blue Blood philosophy is in balance. One example of this balance is its PEPPERCORN SAISON made with Nebraska honey. The peppercorn is present, but it does not overpower; the malt and yeast create a good balanced flavor.

The Blue Blood standard lineup is pretty typical of most breweries, covering the bases of American pale ales, pilsners, extra special bitters and wheat beers. From its main beers and seasonal flavors, Blue Blood is always growing and developing new products for its 10 Series and Outlaw Series.

One specific year-round Blue Blood beer is the 834-HAPPY AS ALE (4.6 percent ABV), an American pale ale that features a slight citrus flavor with late hop additions. This is one of my favorites specifically because it features hops grown right here in the great state of Nebraska. Sourced from a local farm only fifty minutes away, Rhynalds Hop Growers in Prague, Nebraska, the hops are top-of-the-line fresh. We do not think you can have a more freshly brewed beer when the main ingredient and brewing all take place within such a short distance. Talk about farm to table.

The 1327 POD'S ESB (5.6 percent ABV) was one of Blue Blood's first beers brewed. It was named for owner Brian Podwinski, whose love for extra special bitters recipes from his first time homebrewing influenced this particular brew. The 1335 WICKED SNOUT (6.4 percent ABV) is a farmhouse ale named for a Nebraska farm boy. The namesake of this beer worked hard on his family farm, and one of his chores was dealing with the pigs. Those wicked little pigs never seemed to make friends and brought about the name of this beer. With 6.4 percent ABV, this beer will sneak up on you if you are not careful, just like those pigs on the farm.

Our favorite Blue Bloods seasonal beer is the 6-4-3 DOUBLE PLAY PILSNER (5.25 percent ABV), brewed in partnership with the Lincoln Salt Dogs, Lincoln's semiprofessional baseball team. This beer is wonderful to enjoy during a baseball game; you likely won't stop at just one. It's easy drinking while enjoying all nine innings (heck, even into extra innings if necessary). It's awesome to be able to drink a local beer while supporting the local baseball team.

The 1800 BIG LOG WHEAT (5 percent ABV) is the beer to enjoy during the summertime and possibly during a round of golf. This wheat beer is Blue Blood's take on a weizen style of wheat, with great spice notes of clove coming through, making this a great change to your everyday American wheat. Originally brewed for a local golf course, Wilderness Ridge Lodge in Lincoln, the name comes from the huge logs used to build the lodge you see on the can, according to the brewery's website. It's full of flavor and a great drink on and off the golf course. Plus, when the beer is in a can, you can usually sneak in one or two to drink local while you're golfing the back nine.

The seasonal 543-SKULL CREEK PALE ALE (4.5 percent ABV) is another one of my favorites, not only for its hoppiness but also for the fact that the hops grow wildly and are picked locally at Rhynalds Hop Growers in Prague. There is something about fresh hop flavor that just gives this beer something unique. The beer itself is named after the Abie Hop Yard, with 543 being the telephone prefix for the town. Rounding out the seasonal beers are the

467 Ethan's Stout (5 percent ABV) and the Two Guns Brown Ale (5.5 percent ABV), an American brown ale.

Blue Blood Brewing has its standard beers, but it is starting to roll out two new series of beer, the 10 Series and the Outlaw Series. The 10 Series so far has released three varieties: Last Call (8 percent ABV), an imperial amber ale; Pernicious (8 percent ABV), a double IPA; and the Brewerhood (8 percent ABV), a brown ale.

The Outlaw Series, unlike traditional Blue Blood Brewing beers, are brewed and then bottled in 750ml bottles, which are then corked and caged. The beers in the series are new out-of-the-box experimental brews that Blue Blood head brewer Gil and the team are interested in trying. The bottles

Blue Blood Brewing Company has been brewing in Lincoln, Nebraska, since 2011. *Courtesy of Blue Blood Brewing Company.*

describe the series perfectly: "When it comes to beer making, rules are made to be broken. Enter, the Outlaw Series, an ever-changing rogues gallery of highly experimental lawlessness. Enjoy these limited-run beers before the authorities decide to lock 'em up and throw away the key." Available at local Lincoln specialty craft beer shops, this series is great for a weekend barbecue or Fourth of July blowout. They also make for the perfect gift for any craft beer drinker, featuring unique labels made from grain and produced by local Lincoln paper company Porridge Papers.

What's in a Name?

Founded by individuals with strong ties to law enforcement, Blue Blood was a natural name for the brewery. With a large portion of a cop's life spent on shift work, developing relationships and building a brotherhood is inevitable. Blue Blood is a name that allows the brewery to honor the brotherhood, and with no other American brewery directly tied to law enforcement, it was a unique way to set Blue Blood Brewing Company apart.

The name also has allowed for natural law enforcement themes to be weaved into the brands, marketing and packaging. Blue Blood has developed campaigns around common cop terms, and it has used engaging phrases to spark excitement that directly relates back to its products. "You Have the Right to Remain Satisfied" and "Throw the Book at Boring Beer" can be seen across Blue Blood Brewing collateral, and as a consumer, you can't help but laugh and smile.

12

LOOP BREWING COMPANY

404 West A Street, McCook, Nebraska 69001 | 308-345-5198
www.loopbrewingcompany.com | Founded in 2011

THE BREWERY

Born and raised in McCook, Nebraska, Tyler Loop grew up knowing that one day he would open and run a business in his hometown in southwest Nebraska. In 2008, Tyler began homebrewing with the notion that he would eventually turn his new hobby into his full-time job and a local business.

As a new homebrewer, Tyler continued to do online research about his future endeavor and came across award-winning master brewer Tom Hennessy of Colorado Boy Brewing. Tom holds classes for up-and-coming brewers, and Tyler and his wife, Sue, attended the five-day, one-on-one intensive class on how to start and run a small brewery. The training taught them not only the ins and outs of running a small business (employees, products, equipment and so on) but also how to brew on a much larger scale than what his familiar homebrewing techniques could achieve. Tom also introduced the Loops to the idea of "Frankenbrewing," or sourcing equipment for a brewery from non-traditional sources like dairy farms.

With a passion and some training under his belt, Tyler entered the Hormel Business Plan Competition in McCook and came out the champion. With a business plan in hand, $25,000 in prize money and some free publicity, Tyler was ready to continue to source financing dollars and start his brewery.

At the time, Tyler knew that brewing beer exclusively would be just fine, but he wanted this new endeavor to be a full-time job and knew that a brewpub-style business would be crucial to his overall success. As Tyler continued to work on financing, local restaurant owner Adam Siegfried approached him. Adam was already successful in owning and operating a restaurant and seemed like a good fit to Tyler. The two talked about the brewpub idea and became business partners.

With a business partner and secured financing, finding a building to house a restaurant and production facility was next. The duo came across a one-hundred-year-old icehouse only a few blocks from the center of town and along the railroad tracks in downtown McCook. The railroad icehouse that previously brought ice to McCook was a blank canvas and ideal for the business they were trying to build.

After eight months of remodeling the space and building out their production facility and restaurant, Loop Brewing Company opened in November 2011. Keeping the original floor and ceiling and building a focal point around the large windows that overlook the active railroad tracks, Loop Brewing Company is a great mix of the past and present.

Specializing in brick-oven pizzas and appetizers, Loop is mixing up great fare that matches its very drinkable beers, which are sold exclusively in-house. No matter if you are stopping by for a quick pint at the bar or dinner in the restaurant, you're in for a treat.

The Beer

In the heavily agricultural-based community that is McCook, Tyler and his brewing assistants focus on brewing in a way that lets them introduce the community to craft beer and keep them coming back for more. On any given day, Loop Brewing Company keeps a handful of standard beers on tap, ranging from wheats and IPAs to Irish reds and stouts.

The standard Loop Brewing Company lineup includes a pale ale (4 percent ABV), an IPA (5.5 percent ABV), an Irish red (4 percent ABV), a brown ale (5 percent ABV), a cask ale (5 percent ABV), a porter (5 percent ABV) and a stout (5 percent ABV).

When they're feeling really creative, Loop Brewing staff are known to introduce unique flavors and styles—the hazelnut brown, banana stout and the bourbon oak chip–infused porter to name just a few.

Loop Brewing guests can enjoy their standard favorites or try something out on the edge of their comfort zone by the twelve-ounce glass or pint. Or they can join the Lifetime Mug Club and get their own personalized mug that hangs in the brewpub. If beer isn't your thing, Loop Brewing sells homebrewed root beer and cream soda.

While Loop Brewing Company isn't currently distributing outside its brewpub, you can buy a keg of your favorite selection or fill up your sixty-four-ounce growler and take your favorite brew to go.

WHAT'S IN A NAME?

Sometimes when breweries are in the planning stages, they spend a lot of time going back and forth brainstorming unique names for their business. And sometimes the owner decides that their surname is strong enough. That was the case with Loop Brewing Company. After thinking through a few different ideas, Tyler decided that his last name was perfect for his business and just went with it.

It wasn't until Tyler secured his brewpub location that he decided to include the iconic train imagery in his business logo. Being so close to the tracks, and with the structure being a former train icehouse, it was only fitting to pay homage to the history of their new business location.

13

ZIPLINE BREWING COMPANY

2100 Magnum Circle No. 1, Lincoln, Nebraska 68522 | 402-475-1001
www.ziplinebrewing.com | Founded in 2012

THE BREWERY

What do you get when you cross two attorneys and a physician? No, this isn't the start of a corny joke but rather the actual start of Zipline Brewing Company, a craft brewery in Lincoln, Nebraska.

In the mid-2000s, Tom Wilmoth, James Gallentine and Marcus Powers, all successful professionals and lovers of craft beer, started brewing their own beer on the side as homebrewers. They weren't seeing craft beer available in the market that connected with their passion for craft beer and the vision for how they thought it should be packaged and delivered. What they were seeing was something a little more elitist and uninviting. Their vision was to brew beers that were readily available, accessible and easy for even the novice craft beer drinker to understand.

With common conversations between the three including how they would do it and what the beer community was missing, James broached the idea to Tom that they should open a brewery. With no hesitation, Tom shot the idea down. It was not until the two attended a three-day workshop at the Siebel Institute in Chicago that Tom started to come around to the idea.

The workshop included many different classes and provided Tom and James with the basic understanding of how to open a brewery or craft beer brewpub. After the three days at the conference, they both left with the idea that if they could brew great beer, they could definitely handle the operations side of a production brewery. They just needed to decide who was the best brewer.

Tom's homebrewing style was a "get it done and enjoy" kind. As an attorney, there were not too many cases that ended quickly and allowed Tom to enjoy the success. This is the opposite in homebrewing. Homebrewing was a hobby in which Tom could test unique recipes and quickly enjoy batches with friends and family. James, a skilled physician, was a more technical brewer, paying close attention to studying and perfecting each batch. Marcus on the other hand, understood the magic of brewing as well as the technical side of the process; he was the perfect middle ground between Tom and James.

Together, the three possessed vision, technical skill, research and passion, and after finishing up their coursework at Siebel, building out a business plan and convincing Marcus to officially join them in this endeavor, the three went to work building Zipline Brewing Company. In January 2012, they began the business build-out, which included the nuts and bolts of a brewery plus writing, testing and developing their recipes. After ten months of building their brewery and writing and testing more than 160 recipes, Zipline Brewing Company released its first beer, its version of an oatmeal porter, in late November 2012.

Initially, the guys did not intend to lead with such a dark craft beer; however, a local franchisee at Old Chicago in Lincoln, Nebraska, approached them about brewing a limited batch that it could include in its winter beer tour. With six kegs ordered by Old Chicago and now on tap in downtown Lincoln, Zipline's doors were open.

Housed in a twenty-thousand-square-foot building, Zipline Brewing Company is located in an industrial space just west of downtown Lincoln, Nebraska. The space was attractive for establishing the brewery for many different reasons. First, there was plenty of space to efficiently brew (as well as grow), and there was also room for a nice taproom and outdoor seating area. The building is located along a popular train track and lends itself well to escaping the hustle and bustle of downtown. The location was also preferred because it allowed enough distance between the taproom and the customers (downtown bars and restaurants), ensuring that it was not directly competing with them. And while the industrial space presented an initial challenge for

Above: Zipline is located in an industrial area just west of downtown, Lincoln, Nebraska. *Photo by the author.*

Right: The Zipline patio is the perfect escape from city life. *Courtesy of Zipline Brewing Company.*

taproom visitors, it was not a challenge for very long. The Lincoln locals found out about Zipline and have flocked to its taproom.

The taproom, located in the front of the space, was intentionally designed with co-mingling in mind and the goal of creating a place where visitors could feel a part of something and never be excluded. From the mixed-level interior open seating to the outside patio tables and benches, it does not matter your age, socioeconomic background, political beliefs, gender, race or religion; the Zipline taproom is home to all walks of life, with one common denominator: each person enjoys good beer.

The employees who work there represent one of the biggest pillars of the Zipline community. Each employee has some sort of Lincoln connection, and all have a passion for building community and brewing and/or selling craft beer. Many have started at Zipline on the ground floor and have worked hard to learn all aspects of the craft and build the business. Many employees are often promoted from within, and it is definitely a family business. This is even more evident when you actually run into a Zipline family member at the facility—from chipping in with cleaning or organizing, the business has been built on the love and support from the founders' families.

THE BEER

One of Zipline's main goals is to diversify the beer-drinking community and assist those novice drinkers in exploring the world of craft beer. Many beer drinkers often start out by choosing between heavy or lite or dark or light, and once they make a selection, they tend to stick with it. Zipline beers try to open the palate a bit and mix up what people think of when they think of drinking beer. The standard, or year-round, beers at Zipline are all brewed with accessibility in mind and entice those new drinkers.

A few of the more accessible options include the COPPER ALT (5.2 percent ABV), a unique German hybrid between an ale and a lager. This beer is my favorite Zipline brew. It is very drinkable, with hints of hazelnut and chocolate. This beer is so good that I even served it at my wedding. The KÖLSCH (5.4 percent ABV) is another year-round brew that walks the line between an ale and a lager. It drinks like a light lager and is another good entry-level choice—perfect for enjoying on a hot summer day.

The original Zipline OATMEAL PORTER (6 percent ABV) incorporates organic rolled oats and chocolate and coffee undertones. Originally brewed just for the winter months, its popularity made it dangerous to take off the menu; it's one of the most popular year-round options. The NEW ZEALAND IPA (6.8 percent ABV) is a much more accessible IPA, brewed specifically for those who find traditional IPAs too bitter. This beer is brewed to lower the bitterness and bring out the fruit (tropical fruit, blackberry and tangerine) flavors and aromas.

The seasonal selection at Zipline includes the COUNTRY WHITE (4.6 percent ABV), a traditional Belgian brew with a modern twist; it uses a farmhouse yeast strain to create a fruity profile. The Country White is another summer favorite, specifically for Memorial Day and the Fourth of July, and is available from May through July. The India red ale (7.1 percent ABV), available February through April, and the nut brown (5.8 percent ABV), available August through November, round out the seasonal series.

In developing very accessible beers, Zipline hopes that these introductory beers help customers accelerate through their craft brewing experience and reach more adventurous types of beer—like its barrel-aged and small-batch selections, both of which are available exclusively on draft in the Zipline taproom and in a few select bars and restaurants.

While you may not be able to make it to the taproom, Zipline standard beers are available in bottles throughout Nebraska, Iowa and South Dakota, primarily within three hundred miles of its Lincoln-based brewery. If you are in the neighborhood and want to take Zipline with you on your next outdoor adventure, it has a stainless steel growler that fits perfectly in a backpack or day bag.

WHAT'S IN A NAME?

Like any new business at the beginning, you throw around a bunch of different ideas and thoughts on what you want your business to stand for and, ultimately, what you're going to call it. Initially, the Zipline Brewing team threw around ideas about trying something new, getting outside its comfort zone and working toward a better place. Realizing that there is a lot that goes into a name, the team really didn't know what to do.

It wasn't until co-founder James Gallentine built a zipline between two trees in his backyard that the idea started to make sense. After building the zipline and instructing his son not to get on it (as it wasn't complete), his son did anyway and ultimately fell and broke his arm. While this scene

The Zipline logo distinctively features a zipline cord to make up the image. *Courtesy of Zipline Brewing Company.*

is a nightmare for parents, it became a perfect metaphor for the business venture.

A zipline embodies a sense of adventure and the idea of getting on and seeing where the adventure will take you, understanding that once you're on, there is no getting off. Presumably, you will get to the other side one way or another. The Zipline cofounders saw this metaphor as their journey into establishing themselves in the Midwest brewing scene.

14
BRICKWAY BREWERY AND DISTILLERY

1116 Jackson Street, Omaha, Nebraska 68102 | 402-933-2613
www.drinkbrickway.com | Founded in 2013

THE BREWERY

In the heart of the Omaha's Old Market are brick streets leading into and out of the historic area. They take visitors on a journey of the past while winding through to the new modern buildings and passageways. In the center of this historic area, surrounded by bricks, is Brickway Brewery and Distillery, Omaha's first distillery after Prohibition and Omaha's only combination brewery/distillery.

Founded in December 2013 by Nebraska transplant Zac Treimert and then business partner Holly Mulkins, Brickway is the perfect story of what happens when you build something new in the center of a brick-laid path.

For Zac, a former premed major at the University of Wisconsin, it became evident that medicine was not in his immediate future after hearing a local brewmaster share another possible career for a science degree. After he considered a potential life path change, Zac began to look for opportunities to work in a brewery in the LaCrosse, Wisconsin area. At the time, there were few job opportunities at breweries, as active breweries were few and far between. Zac had no luck finding an entry-level brewing job and put the idea on the back burner, accepting a job with Cargill as a chemist.

Once at Cargill, Zac moved to Memphis, Tennessee, and after a few years down south was relocated to Nebraska, where he worked in a microbiology lab on a feed additive for chickens and hogs. It was during his post in Nebraska, and through some family tragedy, that Zac realized he needed to be doing something that he loved: brewing good beer. With his newfound focus, he left his nine-to-five at Cargill and started on the path to finding a job as a brewer.

At first, Zac continued to tinker as a homebrewer, as there were few breweries in the general Omaha area. For Christmas 2001, he had special labels made for his latest batch. Zac gifted the packaged bottles to his family members for the holiday at a family function. His prized batch was held up to lead the family dinner toast, and it was during this toast that some of his family laughed and some cried. It was this experience that allowed Zac to imagine how others would react to his beer. The emotional reaction from something he had crafted sealed the deal that brewing was something he was supposed to be doing.

Coming off the high of his family's positive and emotional reaction to his homebrew, Zac returned to Omaha from his Christmas vacation and started seriously looking for jobs in the brewing industry. He landed one at Upstream Brewing Company in the Omaha Haymarket and served there as an apprentice and, later, brewmaster. After gaining hands-on experience learning his craft at Upstream, Zac decided to further his education in brewing and distilling and moved to Scotland. In Scotland, he enrolled in Heriot-Watt University in Edinburgh and completed a rigorous nine-month master's program, obtaining his master's degree in both brewing and distilling. Heriot-Watt was the obvious choice for Zac, as at the time it was the only university in the world where someone could earn advanced degrees in both brewing and distilling. Zac's passion for brewery was evident, but he was also starting to uncover the idea of applying his same technical and creative skills to distilling spirits.

After his Scottish sabbatical, Zac returned to his brewing job at Upstream and began working on his business plan to open his own brewery/distillery. One of his first actions was working on rewriting the pre-Prohibition distillery laws of Nebraska; this would ultimately allow local businesses to make and market spirits, as noted on the website NewsNetNebraska. The craft distilling bill made it through the Nebraska legislature in January 2007, and by March it had become law, as noted on the website Silicon Prairie News. The new law allowed Nebraska businesses to apply for micro-distillery licenses, granting the manufacture of up to ten thousand gallons of craft spirits annually and the ability to retail the spirits on site.

With the bill's passing, Zac co-founded one brewery (Lucky Bucky) and later sold his equity and opened Brickway in 2013. The idea that beer, spirits and wine bring people together in the good times and the bad is Zac's key to creating memorable experiences. His passion and mission for creating those experiences were critical when he decided what he wanted his new brewery/distillery to do. From that, Brickway was born.

Located in the heart of Omaha's Old Market and entertainment district, Brickway was built on its brews and spirits playing a key role in those friend and family experiences. Brickway opens its doors each day and builds its brand in its street-side tasting room.

The tasting room, located on the main street level of popular Jackson Street, serves as the primary gathering place where visitors can enjoy the latest selection from the Brickway Session Series beers or any of its standard beers always available on tap, including ciders and non-alcoholic favorites like homemade root beer. The space is designed for those gatherings that first inspired Brickway. It features high-top tables and couches for lounging, or you can belly up to the bar and hear about the latest batch on tap from the experienced bartender. Guests have a chance to gather and socialize, play trivia on some nights or tap into the jukebox and dance around to the latest hits. From small after-work gatherings to large bachelor parties, Brickway's mission is to provide great beer and spirits to inspire and fuel memorable gatherings.

Paired with the taproom, the Brickway business is built on brewing and packaging beer and distilling and packaging spirits. The growing production brewery/distillery features a sixteen-foot overhead door that leads to the famous Old Market brick alleys. This door was key in selecting this location, as it allows workers to load and unload supplies using a forklift and other modern equipment to keep up with the demand of distribution. The large opening allows Brickway employees to focus on producing a great product and not waste time relying on human assembly lines to get product and supplies in and out. While Brickway is a small brewery, its space allows it to produce and ship its product to bars and restaurants in the Omaha, Lincoln, Kearney, Hastings and Grand Island markets in Nebraska, as well as in Sioux Falls, South Dakota, and Council Bluffs, Iowa. Brickway is focused on making great beer and continuing to grow.

Even before Brickway's opening, Zac made plans for continued production growth and distribution. In 2012, Zac worked with then Nebraska state senator Jim Smith to help write and testify on behalf of bill LB780 to the Nebraska legislature, according to the legislature website. The bill, which was presented on January 23, 2012, to the General Affairs Committee, allowed

Nebraska breweries to increase their yearly production from ten thousand to twenty thousand barrels. Nebraska governor Dave Heinemann approved the bill on March 14, 2012.

The Brickway family is made up of a small crew of people that work in production and front of the house. Each day, the team delivers the "Brickway Experience," as Zac calls it. Many of the employees have strong homebrewing backgrounds, which is key when it comes to managing the brewing and distilling processes. It's particularly necessary because at Brickway everything is done by hand; there are no computer programs or equipment that alter the processes. In order to keep it craft and keep it local, employees monitor and individually manage each process in the brewing/distilling cycles. Keeping the process close to the people and perfecting its product for people by people is all part of the "experience." Employees pride themselves on not only building experiences for their guests but also taking part in the experience of brewing the product. They know that they have a direct hand in influencing someone else's experience. Whether it's a taproom experience, a brewery tour or a special event, Brickway aims to create experiences for each of its visitors.

THE BEER

Brickway is primarily focused on developing two series of beer, its Session Series and Big Beer.

The Session Series features beers that are 5.5 percent ABV or lower, which allows Brickway to brew beers that are not super high in alcohol but still very flavorful. This series provides an opportunity to enjoy a good-tasting beer without getting too full or intoxicated. The beers in this series include a pilsner lager (4.8 percent ABV). The pilsner is one of my favorite "drink all day and still feel good the next morning" kinds of beer. Whether you're camping, golfing or just getting together with friends, this canned pilsner is convenient and easy to throw in your bag and take with you to any gathering.

The Session Series also includes a Bavarian wheat (5 percent ABV), an India pale lager (5.5 percent ABV), a cream stout (5.2 percent ABV) and a cider beer (5 percent ABV). The Brickway cider beer is another one of my favorites. I often enjoy it after work when I'm just enjoying one or two pints; the apples create a sweet and crisp taste, making it a refreshing beer,

The PILS from Omaha's Brickway Brewery is, to this day, one of my favorite day-in and day-out drinking beers. *Courtesy of Brickway Brewery and Distillery.*

especially when I want a non-traditional beer. While there are plenty of local craft beers available in the Omaha market, there are few local craft breweries with cider beer on their menus.

The second series, Big Beer, includes favorites like the imperial IPA (8 percent ABV), which features great hop character, properly expressing hops and creating a real balance; the imperial stout (9.2 percent ABV); and, as the small batch in the series, oak-aged barley wine (9.6 percent ABV), as well as a rotating specialty. The oak-aged barley wine is full bodied and rich, great

Brickway cans its beers, making them very convenient to enjoy at home, on a hike or on the back nine of your favorite golf course. *Courtesy of Brickway Brewery and Distillery.*

for sipping on—you can't drink too many with the alcohol content being nearly 10 percent.

The Brickway team likes to get creative with its batches and takes advantage of its experience and the opportunity of brewing small batches. The team has fun with brewing batches that could include combinations like half Belgian tripel and half hefeweizen, which matures in a used wine barrel from James Arthur Vineyard (a local Nebraska vineyard) and is spiked with a variety of sours. There's also a half Belgian double, half barley wine. Brickway's infancy as a new business allows it the flexibility to express itself creatively and have fun creating new combinations and brewing easy-to-drink beers that are really fun for customers.

Being the first combo brewery/distillery in Omaha has also had its benefits for Brickway beer production. It has a unique opportunity present in the distillery side of its production and shares space and materials, like maturing a batch of imperial IPA in oak casks that previously matured Brickway whiskey.

In the near future, Brickway plans to continue to work on different sour beer combinations. As a chemist and microbiologist, Zac has been brewing sours for the past ten years, and the Brickway team is always developing new batches. Some of these sour batches can, and likely will, include wild yeast and some bacteria, which without careful handling and Zac's technical skill could be dangerous for consumption.

What's in a Name?

When the brewery and distillery first opened its doors, it operated under the name Borgata, which in Italian means village or town (it was later adopted by the American Mafia to mean "family"). The name played to creating the family

Follow the brick road of Omaha's Old Market to Brickway Brewery and Distillery. *Courtesy of Brickway Brewery and Distillery.*

memories that owner Zac Treimert had experienced with his own family. After a year of business under the Borgata name and a cease-and-desist order from a casino in Atlantic City, New Jersey, the name Brickway was adopted. Being located in the center of the Old Market and surrounded by the original brick roads, Zac knew that this made sense. He contemplated the ideas of Brick Brewery and Brickalley, but unfortunately, both were already taken by other breweries across the United States and Canada. With the original ideas out, the team racked their brains and decided on Brickway, which is another term for a brick alley. The name made sense to Zac and lends itself to their adopted slogan: "How do you do it? We do it the Brickway."

Above: Storz memorabilia beer cans on display at the home of local Omaha collector Bill Baburek. *Photo by the author.*

Left: This Storz in-store display is one of many pieces in Bill Baburek's Omaha beer memorabilia collection. *Photo by the author.*

Jetter's Gold Top Beer plaque from Bill Baburek's Omaha beer memorabilia collection. *Photo by the author.*

Loop Brewing Company is located in an old train icehouse. *Courtesy of Loop Brewing Company.*

Opposite, top: Belly Flop, available between May and July, is the perfect strawberry blonde ale. *Courtesy of Lucky Bucket Brewing Company.*

The Nebraska Brewing Company taproom in LaVista, Nebraska, features twenty-four varieties of NBC beer. *Courtesy of Nebraska Brewing Company.*

Left: A pint of Leatherhead Red Ale at Thunderhead Brewing Company in Kearney, Nebraska. *Photo by the author.*

Below: On any given night of the week, Upstream Brewing Company is packed in both the restaurant and bar. Take this shot of the bar, which was taken on a random Tuesday night. *Photo by the author.*

Above: A peek inside Benson Brewery's slick brewpub in the Benson area of Omaha, Nebraska. *Photo by the author.*

Right: A beer flight at Benson Brewery is the best way to try out the variety of beers it offers on any given day. *Photo by the author.*

Above: Inside the Blue Blood Brewing Company taproom in February 2015. *Photo by the author.*

Left: An employee at Empyrean Brewing Company packaging Third Stone Brown fresh off the bottling line. *Courtesy of Empyrean Brewing Company.*

The core Infusion beer lineup includes a few of our favorites, like the Butcher Block Brown and the Vanilla Bean Blonde Ale. *Courtesy of Infusion Brewing Company.*

Inside the brew house at Infusion Brewing Company in Benson. *Courtesy of Infusion Brewing Company.*

Benson Brewery is often packed with locals looking for a good pint and something delicious to eat. *Courtesy of Benson Brewery.*

Head brewer Rich Chapin at work in the Empyrean Brewing Company brewhouse. *Courtesy of Empyrean Brewing Company.*

Above: Nebraska is known for beer festivals, and Lucky Bucket is at most of them, sampling its latest and greatest beers. *Courtesy of Lucky Bucket Brewing Company.*

Right: In the taproom at Lucky Bucket, you can watch the team brew and see the process that goes into making the beer you're drinking. *Courtesy of Lucky Bucket Brewing Company.*

Paul, Kim and Tyson in the Nebraska Brewing Company production facility in LaVista, Nebraska. *Courtesy of Nebraska Brewing Company.*

Where the Nebraska Brewing Company magic happens. *Courtesy of Nebraska Brewing Company.*

Soaring Wings employees collect money at a Friday night music event. *Courtesy of Soaring Wings Winery and Brewery.*

A shot of the imperial stout, my favorite beer from Soaring Wings. *Courtesy of Soaring Wings Winery and Brewery.*

Right: A Soaring Wings employee pours a pint on a busy Friday night music night. *Courtesy of Soaring Wings Winery and Brewery.*

Below: A Robin Hood Beer "Hits the Spot" illuminated sign from Bill Baburek's Omaha beer memorabilia collection. *Photo by the author.*

Above: Yia Yia's Pizza and Beer in Lincoln, Nebraska, always features a great selection of local Nebraska beers on tap. *Photo by the author.*

Left: A big beer on the SchillingBridge Cork & Tap House patio is the perfect way to spend a summer night. *Photo by the author.*

Above: Chaco Canyon Gold from Empyrean Brewing Company is our go-to ale for barbecues and family gatherings. *Photo by the author.*

Right: The Crescent Moon is Omaha's original alehouse and features hundreds of craft beers. *Photo by the author.*

Above: Swing by the Zipline taproom for a fresh-from-the-tap pint of your favorite Zipline craft creation. *Photo by the author.*

Left: Upstream Brewing Company's original location is located in the historic Old Market in downtown Omaha, Nebraska. *Photo by the author.*

15

INFUSION BREWING COMPANY

6115 Maple Street, Omaha, Nebraska 68104 | 402-916-9998
www.infusionbrewing.com | Founded in 2013

The Brewery

Bill Baburek is no stranger to the beer world. He started collecting beer memorabilia and diving into the history of beer and breweries at a young age. He was destined to be a key player in the Nebraska craft beer game. This avid beer historian joined the craft brewing industry by opening his first craft beer bar more than nineteen years ago in Omaha, Nebraska. Located on the corner of Thirty-sixth and Farnam Streets in near downtown Omaha, Crescent Moon has been the hot spot for Omahans to enjoy craft beer since 1996. It was this bar that led the Infusion Brewery owner to take a leap from selling other's craft beer to opening his own brewery in Benson, a popular Omaha neighborhood.

A beer hobbyist for the past forty years, Bill started his professional career at an Omaha corporation, but after eleven years, he was laid off. With a passion for craft beer, he decided to take a leap of faith and do something that he really enjoyed before applying for other corporate jobs. His passion for beer, which started at age sixteen, led him to open Omaha's longest-standing alehouse. In 1996, this was a pretty radical idea for Omaha. While craft beer was being served in bigger cities across the nation, there was not really a demand in the Omaha market just yet.

Bill opened Crescent Moon with twenty-four craft beers on tap; about half of them had not been previously available in Nebraska. With no domestic beers on tap, Crescent Moon immediately differentiated itself from its competition and was sprinting right out of the gate. With the focus on not being just another Omaha bar, it put all its attention of being a destination for craft beer, and it did just that. It opened with two dozen beers on tap and expanded to thirty and then thirty-seven. And then the whole business grew; it added two more bars to the complex and reached a total of sixty-seven beers on tap throughout the complex. Along with the expansion came a craft beer bottle shop that has six to seven hundred craft beer brands on hand. The corner has quickly evolved to become known as "Beer Corner U.S.A." After the last expansion in 2006, Bill decided that it was time to take another leap and started brewing his own beer.

With a great understanding of the craft beer market and insight into what consumers were looking for, he set his eyes on the up-and-coming Benson neighborhood to house his brewery. The Benson area at the time was being rediscovered. Many down-to-earth independent operators were starting to launch their businesses, and they were thriving. Bill knew that he did not want to open a brewery in Omaha's Old Market or West Omaha. He wanted to be on the ground floor and be in a location with a little grit—Benson had the perfect amount of grittiness.

With some insider info on the old Olson's Meat Market in the heart of Benson, Bill bought the building from a friend and immediately started demolition. Gutting the building but staying true to its original shell, he worked with a local architect to make sure the space did not lose too much of its history. Bill is an avid history buff himself. He wanted to make sure that the building could capitalize on its historical roots and did everything he could to maintain that original charm. When construction was done, he was able to get the building listed on the National Register of Historic Places—no easy task.

After months of construction, Infusion Brewery received its brewer's license over Labor Day weekend in 2013, and immediately Bill and his small team began brewing. Infusion Brewery opened to the public on October 1, 2013.

As a brewer, Bill knew that he did not want to be a restaurateur and did not want to open a brewpub. Instead, he really wanted to focus on developing his product and providing a space to enjoy it. The taproom concept, where visitors can come and enjoy delicious beer and snacks, was perfect for Bill's vision, and it fit well into the Benson atmosphere. Next door to Infusion

Infusion Brewing Company is located in the old Olson's Meat Market in the heart of Benson. *Courtesy of Infusion Brewing Company.*

Brewery is a pizza place, and many food trucks set up in the area at night. Guests are encouraged to bring their own snacks as they enjoy one of the brews on tap. Bill's vision for Infusion was to serve as a local gathering place where people can come and get the freshest beer the brewery had to offer. As a priority from the beginning, the Infusion taproom has continued to be the main focus of the business while it also slowly grows its distribution side.

And the distribution of Infusion is indeed quickly growing; from an initial start of just twenty accounts, Infusion has expanded to about 70 accounts across Omaha and Lincoln. Infusion beers are only served on draft and are available at many popular places across Omaha. You can find Infusion beer at destinations like the Century Link Center and Eppley Air Field, as well as at other businesses ranging from high-end Omaha steakhouses to local dive bars.

With a small team of just nine people, Infusion Brewery likes to keep its distribution close to home and focus on the core philosophy that Omaha and the immediate surrounding area are the best places to be. It doesn't have much interest in shipping its beer too far from home. It just wants to give back to the place it calls home and grow the demand locally. And with a wide range of customers in the taproom whose only shared characteristic is that they like good beer and support local breweries, Infusion is doing a fine job. Benson is the perfect environment for a place like this; it's an indie neighborhood with a local kind of vibe. "It has the perfect amount of grittiness," as Bill would say.

The Beer

With a great understanding of what consumers want in a good craft beer, Bill knew that he didn't want to just brew the same old ale. Instead, he wanted to expand his recipe books and give his guests a unique reason to try his beer. As he was developing his own recipes, he kept these distinguishing factors in mind. A perfect example of differentiation is his porter. The Infusion porter features a special blend of coffee, giving it a nice roasted flavor. Infusion also focuses on being approachable and appealing to those beer drinkers who want craft beer but might not be ready for a Russian stout or double IPA. And while it still has some of the typical craft beers that you might expect, Infusion focuses on providing a wide range of styles.

The core lineup at Infusion features less crazy beers, but they all still have a playful side to them—they really don't take themselves too seriously. The BUTCHER BLOCK BROWN (6.2 percent ABV) is a favorite, with hints of chocolate and toasted malts. I love the taste of hops in it. I used to hate the thought of chocolate in beer, but after trying the Butcher Block Brown, I'm completely open to the idea. This particular beer is also a favorite because it is a nod to the original building's heritage.

Other more standard beers include the RED X IPA (6.8 percent ABV), NO LIMITATIONS PALE ALE (6 percent ABV) and the "Barley Wine Trilogy"— THE GOOD (10.3 percent ABV), THE BAD (10.5 percent ABV) and THE UGLY (11.4 percent ABV)—as well as other stouts and oatmeal red ales.

Infusion focuses on brewing with unique flavors and creating unique varieties, like its most popular and highly recommended VANILLA BEAN BLONDE ALE (4.8 percent ABV). It's brewed with Madagascar bourbon vanilla beans. It's a perfect craft beer for those who might be afraid of craft beer and has a nice flavor and easy drinkability.

Infusion also has more playful beers, like CAMARADERIE BLOOD ORANGE IMPERIAL IPA (8.5 percent ABV), with strong flavor of yummy blood oranges reinforced by citrusy hops. And then there is CHOCOLATE PISTACHIO PORTER,

The Vanilla Bean Blonde Ale is a fan favorite and a must-try at Infusion Brewing Company. *Courtesy of Infusion Brewing Company.*

which is only brewed when Infusion has extra space. It's a milk porter (something Infusion made up), and it adds cocoa powder and lactose sugars, creating a creamy chocolaty flavor similar to chocolate milk with a subtle pistachio flavor. It's decadently sweet and would pair perfectly with two scoops of vanilla ice cream.

It's this type of playfulness and creativity that Infusion is known for. All of the brewers have a background in homebrewing, and they tend to be creative with all the different flavors. It helps that the brewery has a few little fermenters on wheels—perfect for this type of experimentation. Some of the past "experiments" have included APPLE PIE BELGIAN QUAD, S'MORES PORTER and MILK DUD PORTER, along with handfuls of other unique and distinct flavors; these small batches really represent the Infusion brewer playground.

These unique flavor combinations and a focus on developing community through a great taproom experience make Infusion Brewery unique. On any given day or night, you will find all walks of life enjoying a flight at the bar or gathering around a large round table sharing the latest stories of their lives. This is exactly what Bill and the Infusion team focus on: providing a place for Omahans to call home all while enjoying unique locally made craft beers.

WHAT'S IN A NAME?

Names are inevitably the hardest thing to come up with when starting a business. With so many options, it can be a difficult task. But for Bill, the name Infusion was actually suggested to him by a friend; after noodling on it, it was picked because it fits perfectly into their philosophy and business concept. At Infusion, they use a lot of non-traditional ingredients in their recipes. While they still use the typical water, hops, barley and yeast, Infusion's beers are infused with a ton of distinct flavors, from Madagascar vanilla bean and cocoa nibs to blood orange and pistachio. These unique flavor combinations and profiles set Infusion apart from its competition and makes it a unique player in the craft beer world.

16

BENSON BREWERY

6059 Maple Street, Omaha, Nebraska 68104 | 402-934-8668
www.bensonbrewery.com | Founded in 2013

THE BREWERY

Over the past five years, the Benson area of Omaha, Nebraska, has quickly exploded with local entrepreneurs starting small businesses and building a close-knit community, leading to a strong revitalization of the area. Benson has quickly become a destination, with popular nightlife locations like the Waiting Room and Reverb lounge to hot spots like Krug Park and Jake's Cigar. With relatively lower rent, when compared to the Haymarket or West Omaha, and the cooperative environment, the Benson neighborhood area made perfect sense for owner Ryan Miller when he was starting his new brewery. A Nebraska native and homebrewer, Ryan spends a majority of his time in Washington, D.C., but knew that building a brewery in Benson would lead to a great place to come home to and eventually a place where he could retire.

Housed in a remodeled 1910 movie theater, Benson Brewery features warm reclaimed wood floors that are slightly raised like an amphitheater plus modern fixtures and open seating. As you enter the space, it seems more packed than it probably is and reminds you of a bigger city, where space is at a premium. And with the exposed brick walls, big log community table and glass garage door leading to the outdoor seating, Benson Brewery is the cozy neighborhood brewpub that gives you the feeling you're hiding from the hustle and bustle of the big city.

Benson is managed day to day by head brewer Andy Elliott, a Colorado State University graduate with a passion for brewing and degree in food science with a focus in fermentation to back it up. Before falling in love with the Benson area during a job interview and moving to Omaha, Andy spent time as an intern at Odell Brewing Company in Fort Collins, Colorado. During his time in Colorado, Andy had plenty of exposure to all sizes and styles of breweries and was able to gain inspiration for his future business. Translating his experiences from Colorado to the Benson area, the Benson Brewery team has built a community destination brewpub of its own, focusing heavily on creating a great customer experience and providing a space for groups of all sizes to gather.

From the fifty-five seats in the main dining area to the "Hop Box" beer garden that opened in the summer of 2014, there is plenty of space for groups to enjoy a day or night out. Not only does the beer garden provide a great space for a warm summer day, but its ambiance is also community oriented, with long tables and benches set up for guests to enjoy their time with one another. The space is also used to grow hops on the side of the walls and features a planter of barley growing in the back. Neither the hops nor barley make it into the beer, but it's a nice way to show guests the raw ingredients used to make beer, and it's a great conversation starter.

Benson Brewery isn't just brewing great beer. It is a brewpub concept with a classically trained chef, David Meegan, who went to culinary school in New York City and has fine dining experience. David brings his big-city talents to Benson and often cooks with the beers from the brewery, creating complex batters. He strives to source local produce and incorporate it into his menus when possible.

Andy and David often work together to plan unique food and beer pairings, creating opportunities for guests to explore unique flavor combinations. Together they have had great pairings internally, and they've had success pairing with other local Benson businesses. Recently, Benson Brewery teamed up with its neighbor Aroma's Bliss Bakery and held a cupcake/beer pairing. The carbonation of the beer allows you to cut through the richness of the desserts. One combination, an amber beer and red velvet cupcake, was especially memorable. The flavors of the amber beer and red velvet are complex on their own and quite complementary when paired. With notes of vanilla, spiciness and caramel, these two items together are definitely

The Benson Brewery back patio, nicknamed the "Hop Box," is a community escape, perfect in the spring and summer. *Photo by the author.*

something to write home about. Another community pairing that Benson Brewery is looking forward to is a beer and cigar pairing with another of Benson's neighbors, Jake's Cigars and Spirits.

Benson Brewery is not just brewing great beer and mixing up stellar recipes. It's hiring local college students and teaming up with area businesses to further build a strong community. From growing its own herbs in the Benson Community Garden to planting, growing and harvesting its own crops on a small plot of land outside Blair, Nebraska, Benson Brewery is focused on giving back and growing its business by creating memorable experiences and providing a good time in one of Omaha's most vibrant communities.

The Beer

With a small and efficient brewery and no outside distribution, Benson Brewery is a champion of its size, selling two hundred barrels last year in its brewpub alone. To the brewery, its size is an advantage and allows it to be flexible and reinvent itself as often as it wants. With the philosophy that "we would love for you to come have a beer with us," it brews beers like

American lagers to help those who have maybe never had a craft beer before. Specifically, its popular BENSON BLONDE (5.4 percent ABV), a crisp American blonde ale that is easy drinking and smooth without harsh bitterness, is a great transition beer. The WAVES OF WHEAT (4 percent ABV), an American wheat, is unfiltered, light, smooth and rich with a hay-like aroma; it's another favorite of those who are just trying out craft beer for the first time.

While it has those transition beers, Benson Brewery is also pushing the envelope with beers like BERLINGER WEISSE (3.7 percent ABV), a sour wheat ale that is tart with a clean and dry sweetness, and its ALT-ER EGO (4.5 percent ABV), a German altbier with mellow caramelness, creaminess and a subtle bitterness.

Benson Brewery's THE FIX (6.6 percent ABV), an American amber, is aimed at fixing people's perception of what beer should be. This beer features a lot of flavor, piney dry hop aroma and caramel notes, as well as a slightly higher alcohol content—just a few of the attributes that make craft beer unique.

The brewery also knows that its customers want something different when they stop in for a visit, so it has added a few more unique varieties. Beers like the KARHA-T (4.5 percent ABV) is one, and it's not so typical for the average beer drinker. This mild spiced English ale is inspired by a chai tea and features star anise, nutmeg, fennel, peppercorn, vanilla bean, ginger, clover, cinnamon and cardamom. It is definitely not your run-of-the-mill beer, but it is completely worth trying, even if you just add it to your flight like I did.

The BREWER'S DUET (5.5 percent ABV) is a coffee cream stout that features cold-pressed coffee from Aromas Bliss two doors down from brewery; Benson also adds it to its milk stout. It's sweet, robust and has strong coffee undertones. It reminds me of a creamy coffee milkshake, great for dessert or a nightcap.

With its constant creativity at the tap, Benson Brewery aims to always have standard beers available and strives to mix it up and keep its customers coming back. As lovers of beer history, Benson Brewery takes the opportunity presented by its unique capacity and in-house distribution to try new things. Its customers love learning the history of a style of the beer or the story behind the recipe for the beer.

As a true beer history buff, Andy is also exploring brewing beer in an ancient style: via a clay pot, or amphora. Similar to the clay pots used for ancient fermentation that date back to early civilizations, these methods have started to be re-explored, primarily in Europe. With the idea and creative innovation, Andy thought it was time to try it out in Omaha. Teaming up with local ceramic artist Dan Tober, the two designed their own vessels, basing them off ancient styles of pots but modifying them for today's modern brewing processes. Andy is currently souring a few styles of beer with hopes to release them after a year of fermentation. I can't wait to see how this old style with modern twists tastes. These styles of fermenting will likely be the closest thing to tasting the results of the fermentation processes of our ancestors, and that's pretty cool.

WHAT'S IN A NAME?

Coming up with the name for the brewery was relatively simple. The goal of the business has always been to be well respected and a good representative of the neighborhood—a neighborhood with a tremendous amount of pride. So, as an urban brewery in Omaha, it wanted a name that wasn't gimmicky but rather a solid name that represents the neighborhood and the pride it has for its community. With its name, Benson Brewery is able to not only promote its brewpub but also help expand the reach of the Benson community and encourage more people to stop by to discover what makes this place so special.

17
SCRATCHTOWN BREWING COMPANY

141 South Sixteenth Street, Ord, Nebraska 68862 | 308-728-5050
www.scratchtownbrewingcompany.com | Founded in 2013

THE BREWERY

Tucked away in the North Loup River Valley in Ord, Nebraska, is a brewery serving simple beers handcrafted from Nebraska Sandhills water. Founded by three small-town Nebraska boys, Scratchtown Brewing Company set up shop to build a community gathering place where locals and tourists alike could come together to talk, have fun and enjoy locally crafted beer.

In 2008, Caleb Pollard and his family moved from the hustle and bustle of the big city to rural Nebraska to pursue new professional opportunities. An avid outdoorsman and community builder, as soon as Caleb settled in Ord he immediately started dreaming about opening his own brewery. A homebrewer since college, and with his main hobbies being eating and drinking, he knew that one day he would make his hobbies his profession. With the understanding that his homebrews wouldn't cut it for a commercial brewery, he spent the next handful of years in economic development, paying careful attention to economic trends affecting rural America.

With Ord being in the "Great Lakes Area" of Nebraska, with four large lakes within driving distance, plus the world's best water in the aquifer, the building blocks of a new business venture were starting to fall into place.

Caleb knew that he wanted a business that could be rooted in a meeting place for positive energy and fermentation. Then Caleb met Jade Stunkel and started talking about the brewery idea. Together the two had limited brewing experience that would work at the commercial level, but that's where Mike Klimek came into play. A decorated homebrewer, Mike had won contests or placed in the top three at the local, regional and national levels. He also won the 2012 National Homebrew Competition, Indianapolis Regional—first place with his wood-aged beer, Chardonnay Oak Aged Belgian Golden Strong Ale.

The genesis of the brewery started coming together in 2009, but it did not take real shape until 2011, when the three started homebrewing as a unit. Tired of working for other people and letting the dynamics of the economy affect them, Caleb and crew decided that they needed to invest in themselves and take control of determining their own future. Taking advantage of what their remote rural community had to offer, including access to premium water, the three set off with a blank canvas and started to build their masterpiece.

Knowing that a downtown area is the heart and soul of any town, they focused their energies on finding the best space in downtown Ord. With limited existing options and a passion to drive positive change in the downtown area,

Nights at Scratchtown Brewery in Ord, Nebraska, in the Nebraska Sandhills are simply breathtaking. *Courtesy of Scratchtown Brewing Company.*

they constructed their own building on the corner of the downtown square. As stewards of the environment, they were able to build a greener and more economically efficient building. This prime location also allowed them to partner with a number of other local downtown businesses like the farmers' market and downtown restaurants.

As with any business, Scratchtown set out with certain business goals in mind: sustain the Scratchtown families, sustain the brand (the beer), sustain the business (make money), sustain the community (be stewards of driving positive change) and sustain the planet (take care of the environment, especially the water used to make the beer). With its business goals in check, the team was ready to focus on making fantastic beer in a beautiful space, which it hoped to turn into a new community center of sorts, something that was lacking in downtown Ord. By and large, they wanted locals to come to Scratchtown to drink great beer, talk, laugh and come together. They wanted a space that could build human connections.

From educating the locals who had never tried craft beer before to serving the lake-going tourists and the craft beer connoisseurs who actively seek it out, Scratchtown is building a taproom community perfect for the human connections and community building.

THE BEER

Outside of the five key business goals that drive the business, the most important aspect of Scratchtown Brewery is to make great beer, and it does just that. With a simple approach, it carefully takes the four basic ingredients (water, malt, yeast and hops) and formulates complex beers. It believes in brewing beers that are simple to approach but complex in flavor, as well as sessionable and balanced—something you can enjoy with friends.

With a primary local market that is new to craft beer and/or tourists traveling to the lake, their clientele is slowly being introduced to these well-balanced, delicious beers—not beers that will knock them on their butts when they are floating on the river. Beers like the SANDHILLS GOLD BOHEMIAN BLONDE ALE (4.5 percent ABV), HOT IRON AMERICAN WHEAT ALE (4.6 percent ABV) and SWEET SPOT AMERICAN PALE ALE (4.8 percent ABV) are perfect for newbies and lakegoers alike.

The Scratchtown team also brews beers it likes to drink and often brews beers based on the geography and supply chain. It's the goal to source as many ingredients close to home as possible. It sources some grain from Marquette, Nebraska, and it has even started its own hop yard. Some of the area farmers have also even started to grow hops given the new demand from Scratchtown.

Scratchtown has also taken to local events and brewed beers around those. Each year in North Loup, Nebraska (or "Popcorn County, USA"), it celebrates Popcorn Days. For this celebration, Scratchtown brews a cream ale adjunct lager with a corn addition from one of the local popcorn farmers, appropriately named POPCORN DAYZ.

And while the primary focus of Scratchtown is sessionable, friendly drinking beers, it does have some extreme beers, often serving double IPAs to real-life cowboys (spurs and all) and even celebrating the Winter Solstice, the darkest day of the year, with a Dark Beer Fest. On this one day, Scratchtown brewed eleven different varieties of dark beers and paired them with four different cupcakes. The event was a huge success, partially due to the water used in Scratchtown beers being the perfect profile for dark beers. The BLACK EYE IMPERIAL PORTER (8.5 percent ABV) is a great example of a Scratchtown dark beer inspired by Great Britain and eastern Europe. This brew has heavy hints of coffee, and it's creamy and chocolaty and has a rich malty flavor. One of Mike's best beers is the SMOKED SCHWARZBIER, a smoked German black lager. It's a very simple brew, yet the interplay of the malts creates a fantastic flavor that people really enjoy.

With the size of Scratchtown, it has the ability to produce a ton of different styles. In its first year alone, it produced more than forty styles of beer, with a tremendous amount of variety across the board. Scratchtown varieties are best enjoyed close to the source in the taproom, but if you can't make it to Ord, you can find Scratchtown throughout Nebraska on draft from Kearney to Lincoln and Omaha and in twenty-two-ounce bottles in select areas.

WHAT'S IN A NAME?

As you can tell, Scratchtown is extremely community focused, and it makes sense that the story behind its name is a story rooted in local history.

In 1873, as U.S. General E.O.C. Ord was surveying land in the eastern Nebraska Sandhills for the Union Pacific railroads that would be coming through the township, the team was swarmed by biting insects, mainly mosquitos. General Ord and his team were nearly eaten alive, and when asked

The Scratchtown logo features those biting insects that attacked General Ord and his team during the early days of exploration. *Courtesy of Scratchtown Brewing Company*.

what he wanted to name the town, General Ord suggested, "Call it Scratchtown." Instead of going with his suggestion, the town was named Ord after the general.

The story alone has great historical value to the people of Ord and pays great homage to the community that Scratchtown Brewing Company calls home. The name also sounded pretty cool, which helped the name of the brewery stick.

18

PLOUGHSHARE BREWING COMPANY

1630 P Street, Lincoln, Nebraska 68508 | 402-742-0420
www.ploughsharebrewing.com | Founded in 2014

THE BREWERY

Matt Stinchfield spent a majority of his career in industrial cleanup in the desert southwest. After thirty years in the industry, he decided to take his life in a different direction and left the southwest to head for Lincoln, Nebraska. With his new focus on quality of life and vast opportunities to do something new, Matt liked the opportunities that Lincoln provided. He was specifically focused on the proximity to and potential for developing relationships with food suppliers, farmers, ranchers and cheese makers. He saw Lincoln as a prime location. There was potential for achieving more sustainable agriculture in a future business endeavor.

In February 2011, Matt began contemplating the idea of opening a brewery in Lincoln and started building his business plan and digging into the roots of breweries in the area. Although he had no formal training in brewing, Matt had a chemistry background and enjoyed the experimentation side of brewing. With a lot of the process being predictable and systematic, he liked the idea that you could be artsy, flex the muscle of the different ingredients used and highlight the quality of those ingredients.

With a strong interest in brewing classic European-style beers and traditional beers that may not be as well known, his brewery, Ploughshare, had to spend time building in special systems that would allow for these older methods of producing beers. With careful consideration and research, Ploughshare selected a brewery design company from Ontario, Canada, that had a good understanding of the old-school brewing methods and ultimately built out a system that allows for a lot of flexibility.

It was during his research phase that Matt paid careful attention to finding the best place to house his complex brewing system and creating a substantial taproom and kitchen. With strict zoning laws and a desire to be in downtown or near downtown Lincoln, Matt knew that he needed to find a needle in a haystack—something that would allow for both retail and production but not cost so much that he would not ever be able to turn a profit. After one and a half years of searching for the right building, zoned correctly, Matt found the perfect place that would allow Ploughshare to be open late for the retail side of the business, have decent retail foot traffic and be big enough for the production facility—a large portion of the business.

Right in the middle of an industrial and heavy retail area, in an up-and-coming area of downtown Lincoln, Ploughshare found a home along the Lincoln P Street expansion. A current bookend of the expansion project, the 10,500-square-foot building, built in the 1950s, features 16-foot ceilings. Originally a bus and truck repair terminal, the space was perfect, as there were no load-bearing columns in the way and the vaulted ceilings added character to the space. The two-story taproom, plus a small conference room and the kitchen, would take up only one-third of the building, while the other two-thirds were dedicated to the production facility.

After investing his savings, meeting a ton of people to raise capital and securing investors and the perfect space, Matt opened the Ploughshare Brewing Company in July 2014.

Initially opening as just a taproom as they finished the build-out of their very sophisticated brewing system, the brewery pays homage to the past and was built using restored wood from a one-hundred-year-old barn that was torn down near Eightieth Street and Rokeby Road in south Lincoln. The importance of this agriculture tie in is the influence of the past, which plays a key role in the entire Ploughshare philosophy and lineup of beer.

Ploughshare aims to brew beers of the past—beer that is big in flavor and not just big in brand identity or brand loyalty. To Ploughshare, it's not just about the beer it brews but rather the history and vibe of being in the

Ploughshare Brewing Company is located in downtown Lincoln across from the University of Nebraska–Lincoln. *Photo by the author.*

Midwest. It's important to understand that beer is made from agriculture and understand where those ingredients are coming from.

This type of agricultural focus is clear in the food that is prepared and available in the Ploughshare taproom. All of the recipes are tried and true and taste delicious when paired with good beer. It does not matter what brew you choose or what food item you order; the two should pair well together. Ploughshare food ingredients are locally sourced whenever possible and even include the name of the rancher, cheese maker or other producer on the menu when applicable. On any given day, those vegetable growers, cheese makers and ranchers may be visiting Ploughshare and enjoying a pint.

Along with these local producers, the taproom is often filled with an eclectic group of people, from those in their mid-twenties to those in

Ploughshare, like many breweries, offers brewery tours and bike parking, and you can even take beer home by purchasing a growler! *Photo by the author.*

their sixties. Paying careful attention to curating the customer experience, Ploughshare does not attract the typical sports fanatic. The taproom is decorated with the old barn décor, and the background music promotes conversation. Ploughshare intentionally does not play typical modern country or classic rock, and it does not have any TVs in the space. It aims to be a space that brings something different to the community. From bike messengers and college faculty and staff to blue-collar folks, Ploughshare is a place for community members of all walks of life to quench their thirst after work. And while it has a nice menu of food, Ploughshare calls itself a microbrewery with benefits, with brewing being the main focus of the business.

With brewing the main arm of Ploughshare, having an experienced and technically minded head brewer is key to building a program. Ploughshare's head brewer is a veteran who understands how to build recipes and achieve brewing consistency. Being scientific is the Ploughshare approach, and it prides itself on keeping detailed and accurate records. Anyone can brew something well the first time, but without having good records, how are you going to do it again?

Selling beer and making food are also important aspects of the Ploughshare business. With a diverse group of employees, each of the Ploughshare business pillars is managed by dedicated and experienced professionals. From a taproom manager with considerable experience in running an Irish brew house in Denver, Colorado, to a chef/chocolatier from Topeka, Kansas, who has mastered vegetarian cooking and midwestern ingredients, the Ploughshare team is well rounded. The experience is focused on maintaining a sense of community and highlighting local craft beer. And as more local breweries pop up in the Lincoln area, Ploughshare hopes to continue to add to the variety of craft beer available in the area and also add to Lincoln's recognition of being a great place to enjoy a local beer.

THE BEER

Each Ploughshare beer is designed with food in mind, and when it comes to the regular lineup, Ploughshare stays true to the beers of the American ancestors (cream ales) and the classical styles (pilsners) that were brewed at the turn of the century. And while its bread and butter are the classical styles, it tends to get adventurous with its seasonal batches.

Its standard lineup includes the Robber's Pils, a pre-Prohibition pilsner (5.6 percent ABV). This beer is brewed with domestic six-row barley, corn grits and imported lemony Strisselspalt hops. The recipe satisfies those favoring modern Czech pilsners and anyone looking for a smooth, refreshingly bitter pale lager. It's named for "Robber's Cave," a bandit's hideout in Lincoln, Nebraska, that was enlarged with pick and shovel in the 1870s for the cool storage of beers that were quite likely comparable to Robber's Pils, according to the brewery's website.

The Farm Boy Cream Ale (4.8 percent ABV) is the perfect beer to enjoy after a hard day's work. It's lightly hopped, cold-conditioned and smooth. It's one of those beers you don't have to think about drinking; crisp and refreshing, it's perfect for those novice craft beer drinkers.

One nod to the traditional recipe, the Weathervane Belgian-style Witbier (4.5 percent ABV), features 40 percent raw wheat and goes through the nearly forgotten brewing technique of "turbid mash decoction." It's fancy stuff for the beer nerds but fully satisfying for beer drinkers of all sorts. True to the classic examples, this beer is lightly spiced with a secret blend of East Indian spices and fermented with a characterful Belgian yeast strain. It's served naturally cloudy in a tall wheat beer glass, with a lemon slice on request, and topped with a luxurious white lacy head.

To round out the standard series, Ploughshare brews Buckboard Bitter (5.2 percent ABV), an English-style extra special bitter; Tailgate Red (5.3 percent ABV), an Irish red ale; Percheron American IPA (7.2 percent ABV); and the Smithy American Export Stout (6.8 percent ABV).

The adventurous Ploughshare seasonals include many ingredients sourced right here in Nebraska; they are not designed to be gimmicky but rather to highlight the local ingredient, and this adds a really cool aspect to each of the beers.

The First Blush (6.0 percent ABV), a tart cherry witbier, features seven hundred pounds of tart cherries per batch, with the cherries harvested from nearby Kimball Orchard in Nebraska City, Nebraska. The added cherry creates a zingy tart flavor and gives the beer a rosy hue. Each season, the First Blush is available right before Mother's Day and the first Lincoln Farmers' Market and usually lasts until a new crop of cherries ripens in late June.

Ploughshare has also sourced local hops and grain, as well as fresh rhubarb for a Belgian saison and dandelions for a dandelion beer. The dandelions were picked from a two-hundred-acre farm right outside Lincoln, Nebraska, at which pesticides have never been used. This beer, while delicious, was also brewed with the hope that those who enjoy it will stop and think about where their food comes from, as well as learn more about food sourcing and how key ingredients are treated.

Other seasonal varieties include the PITCHFORK TRIPEL, a monastic-style tripel (7.8 percent ABV) available before the holidays and through February. The BUMPER CROP (6.5 percent ABV), a 100 percent organic Belgian-styled saison, is brewed during the cooler months and then held on and made available in late July, similar to the way traditional Belgian farmhouses used to do it. And the COAL TRAIN (8.8 percent ABV) is a Baltic porter (lager) that takes a while to brew. The double meaning of the name reminds Ploughshare of the famed jazz artist John Coltrane's four-disc collaboration with Miles Davis in 1956, the titles of which describe the decoction method used in brewing this elegant beer: "Cookin', Relaxin', Workin', Steamin'." Coal Train is a beer to be savored, like fine jazz.

To stay true to its sustainable agriculture mission and focus on sustainability, Ploughshare beers are only available at the taproom, although it has hopes to distribute in the local market in draft form in 2015, as well as in some limited-edition corked and caged gift bottles. Ploughshare aims to continue to build its local customer following and champions the idea of not forgetting where its ingredients come from.

WHAT'S IN A NAME?

During his initial brainstorming for the brewery name, owner Matt Stinchfield knew that he did not want to link the brewery name to a specific location or some kind of inside secret. Something like Salt Creek Brewing, which would be based off the name of a creek that runs on the east side of town, right past Ploughshare, may make sense to the locals but would not really translate well if the product began selling in new markets. The long-range goal of Ploughshare was to be a well-respected regional brand in the upper Midwest, with hopes to drill deep in the market and not be spread too thin.

With strong ties to sustainable agriculture and traditional-style beers, the name Ploughshare was selected. Ploughshare is the old English spelling of the blade of a walking plough that was traditionally pulled by one or more work animals, either a draft horse or oxen, and driven by a man walking behind it. Early agriculture was accomplished in this way by the homesteaders of the Midwest, and it was this process that allowed farmers to open the land and plant their crops. Like brewing, the plowing process is a long and tedious one, and it has to be precise if you want to have the greatest yield.

19
FARNAM HOUSE BREWING COMPANY

3558 Farnam Street, Omaha, Nebraska 68131 | 402-401-6086
www.farnamhousebrewing.com | Founded in 2014

THE BREWERY

Tucked away in the center of Omaha's Craft Beer Corridor, Farnam House brewing has been brewing locally in the heart of Midtown since 2014. While it has been brewing commercially for just over a year, the owners/brewers of Farnam House Brewing Company have more than twenty years of combined homebrewing experience.

In 2007, co-owner Phil Doerr helped found the South Omaha Brewers (SOBs) homebrewing club; it was there that he met co-owner Tony Thomas. After a few meetings and a few beers, the two realized that they both liked brewing the same type of beers and were both at the same time contemplating opening breweries in Omaha. Tony had an existing business plan that he had written as a senior in college, so the two (along with their wives) started to revitalize that plan and began looking for buildings to house their future brewery.

At first, Phil and Tony were fine with having just a production facility and a possible taproom, but they knew that this setup would only allow them to sell a few beers per visit. With the understanding that Nebraskans like to enjoy delicious food, and with the possibility of sourcing local food and reusing products from the brewery, they decided that a brewpub concept would be best for their business venture.

With the complexities of finding the perfect brewpub space, it took the duo a little over a year and a half to find a space that could house both their restaurant/retail space and an industrial space for brewing. As their search continued, they narrowed in on the Midtown area—or, as they call it, the center of "Craft Beer Corridor." The unofficial corridor consists of the Old Market breweries, Midtown and the Benson area. After a difficult search and a bit of luck, they found their current location.

The building was previously used to sell furs and featured climate-controlled areas for fur storage and fur conditioning. The space was ideal for a bar and restaurant on the main level, and its lower level was promising for a production facility. After calling the owner before he had a chance to list the property, Phil and Tony toured and decided that it would be the space for their brewpub.

Farnam House Brewing Company opened on June 30, 2014, and Phil and Tony set their sights on specializing in styles of beer from continental Europe, mainly Germany and Belgium, while building out a restaurant that complements their specialty beers. To pull this off, they hired Chef Jeff Collins. Jeff, who house makes his own mustards and sausages and even pickles his own vegetables, was the key to building a cohesive brewpub concept. It didn't hurt that Jeff also loved to cook with beer and includes beer (in some way) in about 70 percent of his recipes, including unique recipes for the brewery's spent grain, which he uses in spent-grain pretzels and pizza bread.

The beer selection and food at Farnam House go hand in hand and are directly influenced by each other. The trio collaborate often to develop new recipes for both the bar and food menus. With a diverse menu of beer and food and a knowledgeable staff, Farnam House has grown to attract Omaha's beer aficionados and foodies alike. And while it still has a few items for the beer novice, Farnam House is specializing to attract the more experienced beer drinker.

THE BEER

From the beginning, Phil and Tony wanted to offer the Omaha community something a little different with the beers they brewed. After good reactions to their saisons and farmhouse ales from customer samplings at local beer festivals, they believed that the Omaha beer community was ready for something a bit more specialized. With most breweries starting with English styles, they decided to focus on Belgian, French and German styles and even began to experiment with wild yeasts and sour beers. These types of beers further piqued their interest, and the positive reinforcement from event sampling was a great indication that Omaha was ready for Farnam House's specialized styles of beer.

With its twelve-barrel system (purchased from Thunderhead Brewing in Kearney, Nebraska), Farnam House has a large capacity to try out new recipes and continue to experiment. Some of its experiments have included old-world styles of beer, like the KELLER GERMAN LAGER (5.2 percent ABV). This style is not done too widely in the Omaha area, as most brewers don't have the capacity to lager long enough. However, Farnam House has the capacity and space, and this beer has become a fan favorite and is frequently on tap. Another old-world style is the POLISH GRATZER, which is a 100 percent oak-smoked wheat beer. It's light in body and alcohol but still has tons of flavor; it's great for the summertime.

On any given day at Farnam House, you can find six standard beers, from a GRISETTE LIGHT SAISON (4.5 percent ABV) to the fan favorite, TAFT AMERICAN STOUT (5.6 percent ABV). At the time this beer was being brewed, it was the stoutest beer Farnam House had brewed. Phil's wife and co-owner Bernie thought that with it being their stoutest beer, it should be named after America's stoutest president, William Howard Taft.

From the start, the HOP HARVEST (6 percent ABV) has been popular, and with strong consumer requests, it has become a standard on tap at Farnam House. This particular brew was one of the first beers and features Nebraska hops from DK Knudsen Hop Growers, located outside Fremont, Nebraska. I love a pint of Hop Harvest, with its crisp taste and hoppy finish.

Rounding out the six standards are the BIERE DE GARDE (6.2 percent ABV) and the BELGIAN IPA (7 percent ABV). Originally, the plan was to have only four standard beers on tap, but the popularity of Hop Harvest and Taft Stout led Phil and Tony to keep them on the menu year-round and express their creativity and experiments with seasonal offerings. Some of the most recent seasonals include the RABID REDBIRD BRETT PALE ALE (6.5 percent ABV) and the RUM BARREL-AGED PUMPKIN SAISON (7 percent ABV). If you enjoy pumpkin ales, this is the beer for you. Mixed with just the right amount of spice (thanks to Chef Jeff) and a subtle pumpkin flavor, I get my warm pumpkin fix by the pint all winter long.

With a popular selection of standard beers and a passion for experimenting, Phil and Tony have a lot of beers left to brew and continue to throw their

The selection as Farnam House is full of variety for the beer nerds. *Photo by the author.*

unique spin on things. They have started piloting different recipes using the aronia berry. Every Wednesday, they take a standard beer and add a hop, fruit, spice or whatever is available; brew a small batch; and feature it in the restaurant. Popular Wednesday night batches have included the GRISSETT with Sorachi hops, giving the beer a lemony aroma, and the GINGER BREAD WINTER BACH, for which they again worked with Chef Jeff to customize the perfect amount of spice. Their CHERRY CREEK SOUR was another variety that flew off the shelves once released. Through it all, Phil and Tony plan to continue to introduce unique beers and beer styles to Nebraska. With their current brewing capacity and endless recipe book, I can't wait to see what's next!

What's in a Name?

When Phil and Tony first started pouring their beers at beer festivals, they poured under the name Goldenrod. To them, Goldenrod was ideal for their brewery. But after a cease-and-desist, it was back to the drawing board. After months and months of researching possibilities for a new name, it was the suggestion of a friend and co-worker that led to their current name, Farnam House Brewing Company. When they heard the suggestion, they were excited and decide to go with it.

When it came to brand imagery, from the early days of Goldenrod they knew that trying to draw or replicate a goldenrod flower would be difficult. Instead,

The Farnam House logo features an iconic Nebraska weathervane plus a unique barley pattern to give it the Farnam House twist. *Photo by the author.*

they gravitated toward the weathervane, which in their own words was "quintessential Nebraska iconography." Like their beers, Phil and Tony wanted to add their own twist on things, so they added a barley pattern to the iconic weathervane and have used the logo to represent their brand ever since.

20

KINKAIDER BREWING COMPANY

43860 Paulsen Road, Broken Bow, Nebraska 68822 | 308-872-8348
www.kinkaiderbrewing.com | Founded in 2014

THE BREWERY

Kinkaider Brewing Company is located just a mile outside Broken Bow, Nebraska, a town of fewer than four thousand people in Custer County, Nebraska. One of Nebraska's newest breweries, it's a farm brewery housed on two acres of legal drinking space.

Owned and operated by four native Nebraskans with a combined thirty-three years of homebrewing experience, Kinkaider Brewing, like a lot relationships these days, started out online. Head brewer Dan Hodges and co-owner Nate Bell met on a beer blog in 2005. After a few exchanges on the blog, they found out that they were actually in the same area, Nate invited Dan to a local homebrew club. The two hit it off, so they say, and Dan has been attending the monthly brew club meetings for the past ten years.

This homebrew club, Motley Brew Crew, is also where Nate and Dan met Cody Schmick. Cody moved to the Broken Bow area in 2010, and Nate invited him to the homebrew club. It was at the homebrew club that Nate and Cody had a chance to try Dan's homebrews; they quickly realized that Dan's brews were consistently better than those that were gaining nationwide success. This was about the same time that Nate and Dan started thinking about opening a business in Broken Bow. The area, unlike other small towns in Nebraska, was starting to see growth, and together Nate and Cody thought that opening a business in the town would be smart. The two believed that a brewery would make sense for the area, but they knew that Dan had to be involved. Knowing that Dan's beer was not only strong enough to put Custer County on the map but also something that the town and state would be proud of and get behind, they convinced Dan to join the endeavor.

As with most small towns that were seeing expansion and growth, commercial space for a production brewery was pretty limited. With their thoughts of building new on the town square or close to the highway, Kinkaider's fourth partner, Barry Fox, soon came into the picture. Barry encouraged the group to take inspiration from area wineries and shared the vision of a "farm craft brewery." The vision included housing the brewery about a mile outside Broken Bow on a farm that overlooks the Sandhills. His idea included not only a scenic destination brewery with plenty of space but also the opportunity to be a farm brewery where they could use the land to grow their own ingredients. The scenic space was like nothing else in the area, allowing customers to grab a locally crafted beer, gather and overlook the Nebraska Sandhills. The three partners were sold on Barry's vision; Kinkaider Brewing Company moved like a freight train and in under a year opened on December 26, 2014.

The two-acre farm of legal drinking space is just one mile north of the town of Broken Bow, and while it might seem like you are on the outskirts of town, that's part of the attraction of Kinkaider Brewing. It is an escape from town life, a place where you can enjoy a beer and look out at the Sandhills from the 1,200-square-foot exterior patio; belly up to the bar, which features tap handles crafted from old hedge posts; or relax at one of the many community tables throughout the taproom.

Just outside the brewery, some of Barry's cattle graze, and in perfect farm brewery fashion, all of Dan's spent grain goes out to the cattle. The area also allows for future farming for ingredients such as hops, jalapeños, pumpkins, corn, wheat, honey and possibly even barley. The farming aspect adds to the attraction of Kinkaider Brewing in that some of the ingredients you are drinking could be coming from the land just outside the window.

Kinkaider's philosophy is to introduce new beer styles but also stay creative. And with the community support and backing through the Pioneer Club, it was able to raise about $50,000 in trade, labor, parts and cash, which was a great indication that the community would and was ready to support this business endeavor.

The tap handles at Kinkaider Brewing Company are made from old hedge posts as seen here at Yia Yia's Pizza and Beer in Lincoln, Nebraska. *Photo by the author.*

THE BEER

Head brewer Dan has had a passion for brewing since his early days of homebrewing and joining the homebrew club. Fascinated with the idea that you can make beer from grain and water, he fell in love with brewing and has been exchanging ideas with other local brewers and perfecting his recipes for the past ten years.

Focusing on brewing beers that stay true to basic styles, Kinkaider Brewing Company is also introducing new styles of beer to the Sandhills. As with any new craft brewery, especially in an area dominated by domestic canned beer that has been around for decades, there is a good amount of education needed. Kinkaider is educating the public on craft beer one pint at a time.

Brewing pure unadulterated styles of beers with pure Sandhills water, Dan is brewing up some fan favorites while still working in small-batch and barrel-aged beers to express his creativity. With a ten-barrel brew house, Kinkaider is focused on introducing the standard styles and keeping its taproom taps fully loaded, while also preparing for distribution and sharing its beers across Nebraska.

Some of the beers that Kinkaider kicked off with include the DAN THE WISER KÖLSCH (4.9 percent ABV), a Belgian pale ale (4.2 percent ABV), HERD LAW HONEY WHEAT (4.7 percent ABV), HIRAM'S BONES PORTER (4.8 percent ABV), 4-COUNTY PALE ALE (5.4 percent ABV) and the FRAME THE BUTCHER IPA (6.0 percent ABV).

Dan has also been perfecting his DEVIL'S GAP JALAPEÑO ALE for the past ten years. This award-winning beer has quickly become a fan favorite at the taproom and hopefully will feature jalapeños grown at the Kinkaider farm in the future. Other "mad scientist" concoctions Dan has been experimenting with include a very smoky SMOKED GERMAN ALT BEER and a BELGIAN ALE BLUE SPRUCE TIP beer—this one features the needles of a blue spruce tree. Dan has also brewed up batches of oatmeal raisin cookie– and Almond Joy–inspired beer, featuring hints of chocolate, almond, coconut and vanilla.

No mater what you're having to drink at Kinkaider, you know it's a tried-and-true style, and you will likely find something on tap that you haven't heard of or tried before. Dan and crew continue to experiment and bring new craft beer selections to the Sandhills.

WHAT'S IN A NAME?

Broken Bow, Nebraska, has quite the history when it comes to how the land was settled. Signed into law by President Abraham Lincoln on May 20, 1862, the Homestead Act encouraged western migration by providing settlers 160 acres of public land. In exchange, homesteaders paid a small filing fee and were required to complete five years of continuous residence before receiving ownership of the land, according to the Library of Congress website.

With mostly ranchers and farmers inhabiting the area, 160 acres was limiting and made it almost impossible to make a real living. The Kinkaid Act of 1904, authored by Nebraska congressman Moses P. Kinkaid, was a special homestead law that applied only to the western and central portions of Nebraska (primarily the Sandhills). This act allowed 640-acre homesteads in the designated areas, except for lands set aside as being suitable for irrigation. The act was an effort to respond to the fact that the 160-acre tracts were far too small for productive agriculture and ranching in the relatively arid Sandhills and high plains regions of Nebraska, according to "U.S. Government Land Laws in Nebraska, 1854–1904" on the Nebraska State Historical Society website.

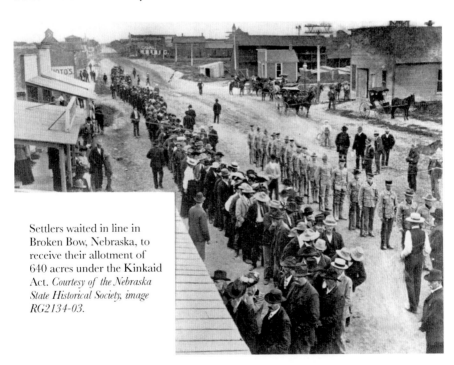

Settlers waited in line in Broken Bow, Nebraska, to receive their allotment of 640 acres under the Kinkaid Act. *Courtesy of the Nebraska State Historical Society, image RG2134-03.*

The folks who received the land under the Kinkaid Act were called "Kinkaiders." The settlers who were filing claims for the 640 acres traveled to Broken Bow to file their claims. It was a mad rush for land, and the lines went all the way through town. The local militia even had to be called in to help keep order.

With a story so specific to the local history of Broken Bow and the surrounding area, and after tossing around many other ideas, the idea of Kinkaider Brewing Company just made sense. It paid homage to the history of the area for those who knew it, and it was an interesting story for those who didn't.

21

SCRIPTOWN BREWING COMPANY

3922 Farnam Street, Omaha, Nebraska 68131 | 402-991-0506
www.scriptownbrewing.com | Founded in 2014

The Brewery

Funny things happen when you meet a friend of a friend. Sometimes these situations are awkward, and other times they turn into amazing relationships and future business partnerships. At least, that was the case with John Fahrer and Scott Stephens.

Introduced to each other by a mutual friend, John and Scott started working together when Scott was opening Lot 2, a restaurant he co-owns in the Benson area of Omaha. Scott had just returned from living in Portland, Oregon, and had an affinity for craft beer. He wanted to brew craft beer at Lot 2, but he needed a brewer. Enter John, an award-winning homebrewer who won a gold and Best of Show at the 1996 American Homebrewers Association, National Homebrew Competition in New Orleans, with his Muddy Moe Amber Ale.

John was just the partner Scott was looking for, so the two paired up. For two years, John and his son, also named John, brewed twenty gallons of craft beer every other Sunday for Lot 2 restaurant. In 2011, John finally decided that he was going to turn his more than twenty-five-year hobby into his full-time job. It was now or never. Again partnering with Scott, the two set out on the journey to open their own brewery. Originally, they looked to the suburban metro area for a place to call home but weren't satisfied. They came across a piece of property in the Blackstone District of Omaha and never looked back.

The Blackstone District, which in the early twentieth century spanned Dodge Street on the north and Leavenworth Street on the south, attracted some of Omaha's wealthiest families. The busy business district was home to many mansions and the Blackstone Hotel at Thirty-sixth and Farnam, and it featured a streetcar line running right through it, according to Omaha.com. The bustling district thrived for a while, but as the wealthy homeowners died and or moved out west, the district perished.

Fast-forward to 2012. The Blackstone District was starting to undergo some serious revitalization, was gaining momentum from local businesses and was once again establishing the neighborhood as a go-to destination.

The two-bay space near the corner of Fortieth and Farnam Streets featured the perfect layout for the Scriptown production facility, with great access for deliveries. It also had plenty of space for a taproom. The building itself featured exposed brick, original wall murals, open timbers and the original pine wood floors. The one-hundred-year-old building had the character that John and Scott were looking for and was a great shell for outfitting it with additional character. They added large paintings of Farnam Street's past, pendant lighting and Edison light bulbs and even a large sliding barn door. The wood barn bar was the main focal point of the space, and handcrafted tables from that same local reclaimed barn wood and chairs made from recycled pallets finished the look.

The taproom was designed to be warm and raw and to allow guests to sit back and focus on the beer. There is no food on the premises if guests get hungry, but they can bring it in from neighboring businesses like the Nite Owl (which delivers) or get a slice of pizza from Noli's Pizzeria or something from Mula Mexican Kitchen and Tequileria—all are only a few doors down from Scriptown. Or head out to Scriptown's back patio and try the latest fare from the Rig food truck, which specializes in gourmet waffle sliders and doesn't disappoint! No matter if you're looking for a quick drink on the way home from work or having a night out with friends, Scriptown is your spot, specializing in session beers.

The Beer

Belgian- and German-style beers with a certain creative flare define Scriptown's session beers. The focus on session beers allows patrons to enjoy several pints in a "session" with friends and family.

Scriptown brews three beers year-round and rotates in five to six seasonal beers, making variety a priority. The three beers always available include the award-winning Muddy Moe Amber Ale (5.1 percent ABV), the Nutjob Brown Ale (4.8 percent ABV) and the Lone Tree IPA (4 percent ABV).

The Nut Job isn't just fun to say; it's a former homebrew recipe of John's and has been the bestseller since day one. Brown ales are usually underappreciated, but this is a great one—I find myself consistently

The menu board in Scriptown Brewery features many beers that are named after historic Omaha locations and landmarks. *Photo by the author.*

returning to it. It's malty and not too bitter; a balance is definitely achieved in this brew.

Scriptown beers are primarily available in the taproom and in limited distribution throughout Omaha and Lincoln. If you are looking for a little kick from beers that pack a punch, Scriptown is rolling out those varieties seasonally, so stay tuned or stop by.

What's in a Name?

Paying homage to its historic location, the brewery name is derived from the moniker of the first subdivision in Omaha in the Nebraska territory in the 1850s. The area was referred to as "Scriptown," as scrip was a popular payment method for the residents.

With the name's roots in local history, a nice sound and a high degree of recognition, John and Scott moved forward with Scriptown as the name for their brewery. Scriptown often names many of its beers after other local historical places as well. The SARATOGA STOUT (3.8 percent ABV) was named for an area of North Omaha. PROSPECT HILL PORTER (6.3 percent ABV) was named after one of Omaha's oldest neighborhoods. SADDLE CREEK WHEAT (4.5 percent ABV) was named for Saddle Creek Road, which runs close to Scriptown. And the GOLD COAST WHITE CAP IPA was named for the historic Gold Coast neighborhood, where Scriptown Brewery now calls home.

BIBLIOGRAPHY

Adams County Historical Society. "The Effect of Prohibition." November 1974.

BeerAdvocate. "History of American Beer." http://www.beeradvocate. com/beer/101/history_american_beer.

Biga, Leo Adam. "Omaha Original Gets New Life on Riverfront Restarting Storz." *The Reader*, September 19, 2013.

Blue Blood Brewery. http://www.bluebloodbrewing.com.

Creigh, Dorothy Weyer. *Nebraska: A History*. New York: Norton, 1977.

Falstaff Beer and the Falstaff Brewing Corporation. "History of Falstaff Beer and the Falstaff Brewing Corp." http://www.falstaffbrewing.com.

Hastings Journal. September 12, 1878.

Jetter Brewing Company. "History." http://jetterbeer.com/history.

Krepel, Terry. "Digging Unearths Keg of 'Treasure.'" (Columbus) *Telegram*, March 16, 1989.

Library of Congress. "Homestead." https://www.loc.gov/rr/program/ bib/ourdocs/Homestead.html.

Lucky Bucket Run. http://www.luckybucketrun.com.

Morton, J. Sterling, Albert Watkins and George L. Miller. *Illustrated History of Nebraska*. Vol. 1. Lincoln, NE: Western and Engraving, 1911. https:// books.google.com/books?id=q2ZBAQAAMAAJ&printsec=frontcover&s ource=gbs_ge_summary_r&cad=0#v=onepage&q&f=false.

Nebraska Legislature. "Legislative Bill 780." http://nebraskalegislature. gov/FloorDocs/102/PDF/Slip/LB780.pdf.

———. "Transcript Prepared by the Clerk of the Legislature Transcriber's Office—General Affairs Committee January 23, 2012."

BIBLIOGRAPHY

http://nebraskalegislature.gov/FloorDocs/102/PDF/Transcripts/ General/2012-01-23.pdf.

Nebraska Liquor Control Commission. http://www.lcc.nebraska.gov.

Nebraska State Historical Society. "Made in Nebraska Exhibit, Breweries." http://www.nebraskahistory.org/sites/mnh/neb-made/brewery.htm.

———. Raw data spreadsheet of the breweries on the Nebraska State Historical Society Registry.

———. "U.S. Government Land Laws in Nebraska, 1854–1904." www. nebraskahistory.org/lib-arch/services/refrence/la_pubs/landlaw7.htm.

Nebraskastudies.org. "The Battle Over Alcohol." http://www.nebraskastudies. org/0700/frameset_reset.html?http://www.nebraskastudies.org/0700/ stories/0701_0124.html.

———. "The Temperance Movement in Lincoln: 'Wets' vs. 'Drys'" http:// www.nebraskastudies.org/0700/frameset_reset.html?http://www. nebraskastudies.org/0700/stories/0701_0123.html.

NewsNetNebraska. "Lucky Bucket Brews Up Nebraska Novelties." http:// www.newsnetnebraska.org/2010/12/13/lucky-bucket-brews-up-nebraska- novelties.

Old Breweries Information. http://www.oldbreweries.com.

Omaha.com. "Business Is Booming in Farnam's Blackstone District." www. omaha.com/go/business-is-booming-in-farnam-s-blackstone-district/ article_82073faf-79ec-50b5-a1c7-871819133584.html.

———. "From the Archives: Cheers for Beers!" http://www.omaha.com/ blogs/from-the-archives-cheers-for-beers/image_567c829b-5c82-5c84- b361-3e27519392b2.html?mode=jqm.

———. "From the Archives: Cheers for Beers!: Habit." http://www.omaha. com/blogs/from-the-archives-cheers-for-beers/article_27ac022b-d1dd- 5c1b-9fe3-9e9a8e8e876c.html?mode=jqm_gal.

Perez, Juan, Jr. "Storz: Company Will Capitalize on Nostalgia, Craft Brewing Movement." *Omaha World-Herald*, August 9, 2013.

Phillips, G.W. *Past and Present of Platte County, Nebraska: A Record of Settlement, Organization, Progress and Achievement.* Chicago: Clarke, 1915.

Ploughshare Brewing Company. http://www.ploughsharebrewing.com/ suds.html.

Silicon Prairie News. "From Craft Beer to Rum, Zac Triemert Tells the Lucky Bucket Story." http://siliconprairienews.com.

Tavern Trove. "Trade Names for the Brewery in 210 Hickory Street, Omaha, Nebraska." http://www.taverntrove.com/brewery.php?BreweryId=930.

BIBLIOGRAPHY

Wakeley, Arthur C. *Omaha: The Gate City and Douglas County, Nebraska.* Vol. 1. Chicago: S.J. Clarke, 1917. https://books.google.com/books?id=niQ6A QAAMAAJ&printsec=frontcover.

Watkins, Albert. *History of Nebraska.* Vol. 111. 1st ed. Lincoln, NE: Western and Engraving, 1913. https://books.google.com/books?id=IkfWAAAA MAAJ&printsec=frontcover&source=gbs_ge_summary_r&cad=0#v=o nepage&q&f=false.

INTERVIEWS

Ames, Josh. Modern Monks. Personal interview, March 15, 2015.

Archer, Dallas. Upstream Brewing Company. Personal interview, March 12, 2015.

Baburek, Bill. Infusion Brewery. Personal interview, February 22, 2015.

Elliott, Andy. Benson Brewery. Personal interview, March 29, 2015.

Engelbart, Jim. Empyrean Brewing. Personal interview, March 22, 2015.

Fahrer, John. Scriptown Brewery. Personal interview, May 26, 2015.

Farrell, Shawn, Tyson Arp, Angela Arp, Kim Kavulak and Paul Kavulak. Nebraska Brewing Company. Personal interview, March 29, 2015.

Loop, Tyler. Loop Brewing Company. Telephone interview, May 15, 2015.

Payne, Jason. Lucky Bucket Brewing. Personal interview, February 2, 2015.

Podwinski, Brian. Blue Blood Brewing Company. Telephone interview, February 21, 2015.

Pollard, Caleb. Scratchtown Brewery. Personal interview, May 2, 2015.

Schaben, Trevor. Thunderhead Brewing. Personal interview, April 27, 2015.

Schilling, Sharon, and Dallas Schilling. SchillingBridge. Personal interview, March 18, 2015.

Schmick, Cody. Kinkaider Brewing. Personal interview, March 1, 2015.

Shaw, Jim. Soaring Wings. Personal interview, April 25, 2015.

Spilker, Sam. Spilker Ales. Personal interview, March 16, 2015.

Stinchfield, Matt. Ploughshare Brewing Company. Personal interview, February 23, 2015.

Thomas, Tony. Farnam House Brewing. Personal interview, March 30, 2015.

Triemert, Zac. Brickway Brewery and Distillery. Personal interview, January 27, 2015.

Wilmoth, Tom. Zipline Brewing. Personal interview, March 7, 2015.

INDEX

INDEX

INDEX

ABOUT THE AUTHOR

An avid iPhone food photographer and French fry connoisseur, Tyler Thomas is a self-proclaimed foodie and the co-founder and managing editor of the Nebraska-based food blog nebraskafoodie.com. The blog focuses on exploring and showcasing the culinary wonders from across the state, shining a light on Nebraska's ever-changing local culinary scene. With a passion for exploring small towns, big cities and Nebraska villages, Tyler tells the stories of local entrepreneurs through blogging and photographing his experiences. Tyler and his wife, Mandy, are based out of Lincoln, Nebraska.